MUSHROOMS
FOR THE
MILLIONS

by
JOHN WRIGHT

Read Country Books
Home Farm
44 Evesham Road
Cookhill, Alcester
Warwickshire
B49 5lJ

www.readcountrybooks.com

ISBN No. 978-1-40679756-5

British Library Cataloguing-in-publication Data
A catalogue record for this book is available
from the British Library.

Read Country Books
Home Farm
44 Evesham Road
Cookhill, Alcester
Warwickshire
B49 5lJ

www.readcountrybooks.com

MR. BARTER'S MUSHROOM GROUNDS.

MUSHROOMS FOR THE MILLION.

ILLUSTRATED

A PRACTICAL TREATISE

ON THE CULTIVATION OF THE

MOST PROFITABLE OUTDOOR CROP KNOWN

BY

JOHN WRIGHT,

Assistant Editor of the " Journal of Horticulture and Home Farmer."

LONDON:
171, FLEET STREET, E.C.
1883.

PREFACE.

In compliance with numerous and pressing requests (apart from the after-noted initial suggestion of Mr. Thomas, late gardener to Sir Robert Peel, Bart., now at Impney Hall, Droitwich), the articles on Mushroom culture in the open air, which were recently published in the *Journal of Horticulture*, are embodied in this small treatise, with several additional chapters to render the work more complete and useful. I am compelled to add that during the passage through the press of the articles in question so many letters were received, and are still arriving, that it is impossible to answer them by post. Those readers of this treatise, however, who may need further cultural particulars can, if they desire, have them through the correspondence columns of the Journal in which the greater portion of the essay originally appeared, provided they state their wants clearly and concisely. Already I have the satisfaction of knowing that my endeavours to impart information on the cultivation of this profitable crop have not been fruitless, several examples of success being recorded that cannot be cited here; others will follow if the simple instructions detailed in the work are strictly and intelligently carried out. The best time for beginners to collect manure for outdoor Mushroom beds is towards the end of July. In three weeks it will be ready for forming into beds or ridges, in another week spawn may be inserted, eight weeks afterwards Mushrooms will appear, and the beds will continue productive for three months. Thus, broadly stated, there is one month of working, two of waiting, and three for gathering the crops.

J. W.

London, May 1st, 1883.

PREFACE TO THE SECOND EDITION.

—◇◇◇—

THE rapid sale of this treatise has proved its accepta-
bility, the first edition having been exhausted in a few
weeks. To the many flattering notices of the work in the
press, and the approval of cultivators of great reputation,
this result is mainly due, and the kindly references of
all are much appreciated. The present edition being of a
more substantial character than the former, is also more
complete, hence it is hoped will not be less welcome, and
especially as it appears in time for the culture of the
important crop on which it treats.

J. W.

London, September 10th, 1883.

CONTENTS.

MUSHROOMS FOR THE MILLION.

INTRODUCTION.

THE following letter, dated November 1st, 1881, has been communicated by Mr. Thomas, gardener to Sir Robert Peel, Bart., of Drayton Manor Gardens, Tamworth, enclosing one, which appears on page 14, from Mr. Barter, who is an extensive and successful grower of Mushrooms for Market on beds in the open air :—

"I have lately had a correspondence with Mr. J. F. Barter, of Portland House, Lancefield Street, Harrow Road, London, W., who earns a living entirely by Mushroom-growing and spawn-making, which business he tells me he has followed for seven years. Last year it appears he grew over two tons of Mushrooms for Covent Garden Market. He grows them all out of doors, and, for all last winter was such a severe one, he only missed picking during one week, which was the famous Black Tuesday week. If his experience were embodied in a pamphlet I feel sure a great impetus might be given to Mushroom-growing (in the neighbourhood of towns especially), which might grow into an important industry. Instead of importing Mushrooms I see no reason why we should not export them instead. He mentions that they can be grown to pay at or above 4d. per lb.; it is easy now to obtain 1s. 6d. per lb. or more."

In accordance with the above suggestion I have been requested to treat the subject as fully as a somewhat lengthened experience of the work and great facilities for observing the work of others enable me to do. In complying I propose taking a broad view of the matter, and prefer to regard the crop under notice as one which the greatest possible number can have a share in growing and enjoying, rather than being content to consider it as a luxury for the affluent, who alone obtain a more or less adequate supply.

When we say that the Mushroom ranks amongst the

most esteemed esculents : that it is one of the most
delicious and at the same time is highly nutritious—
that it, in fact, approaches nearer to animal food than
any other vegetable does : that the supply generally is
quite inadequate to the demand, and that Mushrooms
can be grown in nearly every village and in the suburbs
of almost all cities and towns in this country, we must
at once concede that their increased cultivation is
highly desirable, and the more so since no vegetable
nor fruit crop will give equal returns to the cultivator
off a given plot of ground, say from 20 square yards in
extent to an acre. As this may appear to some readers
a bold statement, it will be well to show that it is in
no manner exaggerated by proving that every part of
our thesis is true.

Few, it is presumed, will dispute the accuracy of the
first sentence of our proposition relative to the public
estimate of the Mushroom. It is generally admitted
that the taste for some fruits, the Tomato for instance,
has to be acquired, and it is the same in regard to
some of the Fungi—to wit, the Truffle ; but the taste
for Mushrooms appears established, almost inherent,
or at least if it has to be acquired it is usually accomplished in one or two very short lessons. The truth
is, the flavour of the Mushroom commends itself to all
palates, or nearly all, as readily as any other dish does
that is prepared for the table ; but who will say that
all palates can be gratified, and the wants of all would-
be-consumers of Mushrooms met in any substantial
manner, except perhaps sometimes during one month
out of the twelve, when the pastures happen to yield
a plentiful supply ? As it is impossible that this question can be answered in the affirmative we arrive at
the fact—a twin fact we may term it—that the taste
for the Mushroom is firmly established, but with the
present inadequate and fitful supply it cannot be nearly
satisfied.

Instead of the great body of consumers being dependant on the weather for a supply of Mushrooms during
the short period indicated, an endeavour will be made to
show how they may be obtained in sufficient quantity
for all culinary purposes during more than two-thirds

of the year, and that cultivators of them who make themselves proficient will reap a rich reward for their labour.

NUTRITIVE PROPERTIES OF MUSHROOMS.

It has been said that the Mushroom approaches nearer to animal food than does any other vegetable. This is proved by analyses. "Although," says Professor Church in his excellent manual "Food" (Chapman & Hall), "the value of cryptogamic plants generally as food is ill understood; and especially is the real nature of several kinds of fungi, which have been eaten safely, still in some measure doubtful; yet a delicate and agreeable flavour is possessed by Mushrooms, and their chief constituents have been ascertained as follows :—

	In 100 parts.	In 1 lb. ozs. grs
Water	90·0	14 175
Albuminoids, &c.	5·0	0 350
Carbohydrates, &c.	3·8	0 266
Fat	0·7	0 49
Mineral Matter	0·5	0 35

The same authority also states that "Mushrooms when dry contain half their weight of nitrogenous matter," its exact nature, however, and feeding value not being precisely known. But what is known is that no other vegetable contains so much flesh-forming material as this esculent, while it is not deficient in heat-givers and has mineral matter in abundance.

At the first glance at the above table inexperienced readers may naturally conclude that no product can be very nutritious which contains 90 per cent. of water ; but they must remember that Mushrooms are not intended to be eaten alone, nor are they so eaten, and when accompanied with bread, so far from the water being excessive, it is insufficient for the wants of man. Even meat, it must be borne in mind, often contains 75 per cent of water, while average cows' milk contains 86 · per cent. and skimmed milk 89 per cent. Many vegetables also contain more water than Mushrooms do, while they do not possess nearly the same amount of

heat-giving and flesh-forming properties—notably Celery,
Lettuce, Seakale, Vegetable Marrows, Turnips, Cabbages,
Onions, Cucumbers, and Rhubarb ; therefore the
nutritive value of the Mushroom must not be prejudiced
by its large per-centage of water. Relative to this
phase of the subject it will not be inappropriate to sub-
mit from the eminent authority above quoted the following average daily ration for maintaining an average-sized
man in health :—

	In 100 parts.		Each 24 hours. lbs. ozs. grs.		
Water	81·5	....	5	8	320
Albuminoids, or flesh-formers	3·9	....	0	4	110
Starch, Sugar, &c.	10·6	....	0	11	188
Fat	3·0	....	0	3	337
Common salt	0·7	....	0	0	325
Phosphate, potash salts, &c.	0·3	....	0	0	170

It will thus be seen that of the total daily ration of just
under 7 lbs. more than $5\frac{1}{2}$ lbs. consist of water. Compared, then, with some other vegetables, and also with
what may be termed this test table, the Mushroom
appears to rank as an important as it is certainly a
delicious article of food.

It is beyond doubt that many enjoyable and not
unwholesome meals are had in which Mushrooms, when
Nature provides them bountifully, form the principal
adjunct to bread ; and it is equally certain that thousands more would be provided were Mushrooms as plentiful as they might be and cheaper than they now are.
For various culinary purposes they are, apart from
forming the staple of a repast, also indispensable, but
only the favoured few obtain sufficient for their wants.
Mushrooms, then, are nutritious, and their increased
cultivation is desirable. It must now be shown that
they can be grown in nearly every village and in the
suburbs of all cities and towns.

MEANS FOR GROWING MUSHROOMS.

Vast numbers of persons who have the means for
growing Mushrooms never attempt their culture, presumably because of the supposed necessity of costly
structures and of the existence of some mystery per-

taining to the culture of the crop. Costly structures are not necessary for the growth of Mushrooms on either a large or small scale, nor is there any profound mystery attaching to their culture. On the contrary, elaborately built and too highly heated structures have in not a few cases led to failure, while the extraordinary care that has been taken in preparing the beds for this very simple but supposedly mysterious crop has had the certain effect of defeating the object of the cultivator. So far from expensive houses being requisite for Mushroom culture, neither houses, nor sheds, nor cellars, nor lofts, nor caves are indispensable. That Mushrooms are grown in houses and other enclosures above and below ground is true, and most valuable good Mushroom houses are, even essential, in the gardens of the affluent. Where a regular and unbroken supply—a given quantity—has to be provided daily an increase of temperature is occasionally requisite, and forcing to a greater or less extent has to be resorted to. Under those circumstances good Mushroom houses are important adjuncts of gardens, and the more so since they can be, and are, employed for advancing other crops, such as Seakale, Rhubarb, and blanching salads. Without, then, saying anything against Mushroom houses, but, on the contrary, admitting their usefulness, it must still be asserted in the most firm and unequivocal manner that Mushrooms in abundance can be grown from September to June, both months included, without the aid of any building whatever, and the best proof of the accuracy of this assertion is the fact that a far greater quantity are grown on beds in the open air during the period named than are produced in all the houses, sheds, and cellars in Britain. At a moderate estimate 3 tons of English-grown Mushrooms are sold in Covent Garden weekly, gathered from beds made in the open air in the neighbourhood of London, and a considerable quantity also comes from the caves in France.

CULTURE IN THE OPEN AIR.

As an example of the open-air system of Mushroom culture the routine of what may be termed a Mushroom farm in the western district of the metropolis may be adduced. Mr. J. F. Barter's reputation as a manufacturer of Mushroom spawn has long been established, but it was not so widely known until recently, by his exhibitions at South Kensington, that he is equally successful as a grower of Mushrooms for the million. The details of his method of culture, therefore, cannot fail being instructive, and the results he has achieved ought to encourage others who have better means for carrying out the practice than he has to engage in the same work and persevere until they succeed. They will then prove for themselves the truth of the statement that "no vegetable nor fruit crop will give equal returns to the cultivator off a given plot of ground ;" and they will at the same time provide the inhabitants of populous districts with what they certainly do not now possess—an adequate supply of this much-coveted and important esculent. It is self-evident, too, that Mushrooms can be grown in nearly every village and in the suburbs of almost all cities and towns, for the crude materials are there—horses and soil—and only intelligent labour is requisite to turn them to profitable account. As mere statements, however, relative to the remunerative character of Mushroom culture cannot be expected to convince the public, facts must be adduced, and figures founded on those facts, the accuracy of which anyone may test for himself. Then, if the results astonish him and he cannot accept the grounds on which the figures are based, only one alternative can be suggested—namely, that he do what the writer has done—seek the privilege of seeing the Mushrooms gathered and weighed, and form his own conclusions on the subject.

COMPARATIVE PROFITS OF OUTDOOR CROPS.

HAVING shown, what will not be disputed, that Mushrooms are highly esteemed because they are delicious ; also that they are nutritious and constitute an important article of food ; further, that the supply is quite inadequate to the demand that exists for them in the great centres of population, and lastly that they can be grown indoors or out in every district of the kingdom where horse stable manure is plentiful, and skill is provided or may be created to use it rightly, endeavour must now be made to show the accuracy of the statement that has been made relative to the remunerative character of the crop. It has been asserted that in this respect it exceeds all others that can be grown in fields or gardens for purposes of consumption, the cultivation of choice plants and flowers, and raising valuable seeds, being so special that they are not fairly eligible for comparison ; but such crops as are eligible are hardy fruits of various kinds and vegetables. First, then, the average value per acre of several crops shall be approximately adduced, and it will be seen that the remunerative character of Mushrooms surpasses them all.

VALUE PER ACRE OF FRUITS AND VEGETABLES.

In submitting the following figures it is necessary to say that they are founded on the average results that have been realised over a series of years. In some districts certain crops may exceed the amounts per acre, but during other years the majority of crops will by no means equal the values apportioned ; indeed, during some seasons there are both vegetable and fruit

crops that afford no profit to the cultivator. This has
been the case with much land devoted to fruit during
recent years, and not less so in regard to many vegetables. The severe frosts of winter have destroyed
many of the latter, while such summer and autumn crops
as Peas, Kidney Beans, Savoys, &c., have so far exceeded
the demand as to be unsaleable at prices that would
even fairly remunerate the growers, as many of them
know to their cost. The advice that is so frequently
given, with the best possible intentions, to farmers to
grow green vegetables for market on their farms is
neither safe nor sound, unless it is limited to those in
specially favoured districts. These remarks are necessary, alike because they pertain to a subject of national
importance, and because without some such explanation
as they convey, the undermentioned estimated values
might be deemed too low. Fruit crops, like vegetables,
are also affected by the disastrous effects of spring frosts ;
but over an average of seasons fruit culture is doubtless
profitable, and the more certain to be so when different
kinds are grown, as they seldom all fail together.
Under all the circumstances the average values given
are believed to be rather too high than too low ; and
they certainly have not been fixed with the object of
presenting more favourably the relatively greater value
of Mushrooms. By way of adducing proof of the
absence of any such desire, some extreme prices that
have very occasionally been realised for certain crops
and recorded as extraordinary shall be adduced, and it
will be seen that even as compared with these the profits
resulting from a simple yet well-conducted system of
Mushroom culture are enormously greater than can be
derived from any other farm or garden crop that is
grown in the open air in this country.

In estimating the value per acre of different produc-
tions, we will first take the fruit crops. Cherries may
be valued at (or as fluctuating between) from £20 to £40
per acre ; Filberts, £30 to £50 ; Gooseberries, £20 to
£30 ; Black Currants, £30 to £40 ; Red Currants, £20
to £30 ; Strawberries, £10 to £50 ; Raspberries, £20 to
£40 ; Apples, £20 to £40 ; and Plums, including
Damsons, at £25 to £40 per statute acre.

The following may be taken as nearly as can be obtained fair average values of some of the principal vegetable crops—Potatoes (early), £20 to £30 ; Cabbages (early) £40 to [£50 ; Lettuces, £10 to £40 ; Peas, £10 to £30 ; Kidney Beans, £10 to £20 ; Onions, £20 to £40 ; Cucumbers, £10 to £20 ; Brussels Sprouts, £10 to £30 per statute acre. It must be remembered, however, that stated in this form the value of the land under vegetable crops is not fully rendered. Land devoted to fruit-production can only yield one crop in a year ; but under skilful management two or even three crops of vegetables are produced ; but ordinary farmers cannot be expected to produce them, and until they can they will often find fields of green vegetables unprofitable ; but even under the best system of double cropping and allowing to each of the crops the full average value, they in combination do not approach the amount derivable, and which has frequently been derived and is regularly obtained from Mushrooms occupying the same extent of ground.

Now as a still stronger comparative test of the profits of Mushroom-growing some extreme prices that have been realized for other crops shall be adduced—namely, £100 per acre for very early Potatoes; £192 for Onions ; £100 for early Cos Lettuces ; £100 for Plums ; £100 for Gooseberries ; £150 for Strawberries ; £168 for Black Currants, and £200 per statute acre for Filberts. Tomatoes may also be included, although the crop is now extremely uncertain in consequence of the prevalence of the disease that often so seriously affects them, and not unfrequently renders the crops worthless. Still in a favourable season as much as £300 per acre can be obtained from a crop of Tomatoes in the open air. Even these "extraordinary" prices are far exceeded by a well-managed system of outdoor Mushroom culture.*

---

* The average estimated values of fruit and vegetables have been obtained directly from large cultivators in Kent and Essex, and confirmed by an experienced salesman of garden produce in London. The "extraordinary" prices have been chiefly derived from Burbidge's "Industry of Horticulture." (Stanford, Charing Cross.)

A CAUTION TO FARMERS.

The prices enumerated above may possibly tempt some holders of land to devote it to vegetable culture even if they have had no experience in the work. Let them pause before changing their system. Unless they are so situated that they can be first in the market with superior produce they must not expect to obtain anything like even the average prices quoted, and their greatest chance of success lies in the cultivation of such root crops as early Potatoes, Onions, Carrots, Parsnips, and similar crops where the land and situation are favourable for their culture. Before entering on the wor of vegetable farming let the inexperienced consider that salesmen and greengrocers have to be reckoned with. At present these individuals, especially the latter, derive the greatest profits from vegetable culture. Let them also remember that the weather is as much likely to injure or even ruin green vegetable crops as it is to affect injuriously the cereal and ordinary root crops of the farm ; and let them further understand that even the most experienced market gardeners cannot anticipate the nature of the supply and demand a year in advance, and when they attempt to do so they sometimes make great mistakes and incur serious loss. One instance of this will suffice. In 1878 Scarlet Runner Beans were scarce, and the seed did not ripen well. What so likely as that after a barren harvest of seed the following year's crop would be limited, and the prices for Beans consequently high ? Everybody thought there would be few Beans sown because of the scarcity of seed, and everybody made special effort to obtain seed, and it appears did obtain it at a high price. The result was that a greater acreage than usual was placed under this crop, and the summer and autumn being favourable for the growth and fruiting of the plants the supply of produce so far exceeded the demand that tons of fine fleshy pods did not realise more than sufficient to defray the railway charges and the agents' commission. Hundreds of pounds were lost to the growers by this one crop. It is only fair to farmers who are urged to become market gardeners that they should be acquainted with contingencies of this nature, and to the losses to which cultivators are liable. It is not the fashion now-a-days to enunciate a doctrine of this kind, but when there is a danger of industrious men being mislead by kindly advice "fashion" must be ignored, and both sides of an important question must be fairly represented. The only advantage farmers may possess over market gardeners or growers of vegetables is that the former can feed their stock with the produce that cannot be profitably disposed of in the markets ; and it is the fact that many acres of vegetables that were produced at great cost have been so disposed of in Kent, on the principle of choosing the lesser of two evils. "But," it may be very naturally urged, "if a caution is needed against indiscriminate vegetable-growing under the temptation of high prices, there is at least equal need for caution against a similar rush into Mushroom-growing if the prices that have been obtained are considerably higher." This is true, and when some facts, startling facts they will be to some readers, have been presented on Mushroom culture, a word of caution will follow, and a possible danger ahead will be fully and fairly discussed, the object being to guide safely, not to mislead.

THE MOST REMUNERATIVE OUTDOOR CROP KNOWN.

As there is no small number of individuals who are deeply impressed with the idea that anything can be proved by figures, and that crops recorded of unusual value are only grown "on paper," it is necessary to say that the following figures are not evolved from any fanciful theory or scheme by which the amount they represent might be obtained, but they express what has been accomplished, and this not by chance in any particular season, but as embodying the results that have been produced every season during the past seven years. In a word, the Mushrooms that have been gathered, weighed, and sold, and the amount that has been actually realised, can only be fairly represented by the figures now to be submitted, and any others would be incorrect. They are founded on the well-ascertained fact that a lineal yard of Mushroom bed in the open air yields produce of the value of 15s., and that the cost of production is 5s. per lineal yard. This, it must be remembered, is the average yield as ascertained by the crops gathered and sold during a series of years. Occasionally when an extraordinary crop has been produced at a time when the market price for Mushrooms was high the returns from beds have been 45s. per lineal yard. This is mentioned as evidence that no attempt has been made to estimate the average value as greater than it really is. And now the basis having been given on which the figures are founded, their accuracy can be tested by such facts as will be adduced for that purpose, and it will be found that the profits of a well-conducted system of Mushroom culture, which will be described, have not been over-estimated.

It should be stated that the average price of Mush-

rooms sold by auction in Covent Garden Market during
the past seven years is just 1s. per lb.—that is to say,
that this is the amount that has been received by Mr.
Barter, after deducting salesman's commission, during
that period. Occasionally, when very plentiful, only
8d. per lb. has been returned, but on other occasions the
salesman's returns to the grower have been 1s. 9d. per
lb.; the actual average is, however, as stated, 1s. per
lb., and this simplifies the matter of calculation.

COST AND PROFITS OF MUSHROOM CULTURE.

It will be well first to refer to their culture on a
small scale, or as confined to one bed 2½ feet wide at
the base and 30 yards long. "For making a bed of
this extent," writes Mr. Barter, "twenty loads of fresh
manure are needed. The cost of this at 3s. 6d. per load,
the price at which it is delivered, is £3 10s. The cost
of labour—a heavy item—for preparing the manure,
making the beds, gathering and marketing the Mushrooms—indeed, everything, is £5 10s., or a total of £9
for the 30 yards. The value of the produce at 15s. per
yard is £22 10s., and the manure when decayed is sold
for £1 10s.—that is, twelve loads at 2s. 6d. per load, or
just 1s. per yard run of bed. I therefore derive a
profit of £15 from a length of bed of 30 yards." This,
it must be remembered, is the profit that is maintained
throughout the season from a series of beds reaching
in the aggregate to about half a mile in length, the
price being averaged, because actually realised, at 1s.
per lb. The price obtained is often much higher, and
a yard of bed frequently yields much greater weight
than 15 lbs. of Mushrooms. For instance, a bed 20
yards long yielded 160 lbs. at one gathering, and another
25 yards long gave at the first gathering 76 lbs., the
second 200 lbs., and the third 84 lbs., or 360 lbs. in
three weeks; and the same bed continued productive
for at the least five weeks longer. It is necessary to
state these facts as showing that the value of a bed 30
yards long has not been exaggerated. A glance at the
engraving on the frontispiece of Mr. Barter's Mushroom
grounds, from a sketch made in January, 1882, will

suffice to show that Mushroom-growing for market is no myth, and that ample scope is afforded for arriving at an accurate judgment relative to the costs and profit of the culture of the popular esculent on a large scale is indicated in the following letter written in the autumn of 1881.

MR. BARTER'S LETTER AND EXPERIENCE.

" For producing a ton of Mushrooms I consider a hundred cartloads of manure are required. For this, just as it comes from the stables, I pay 3s. 6d. per load, stacked square 2½ feet above the top of a full-sized cart. In the way in which I use it two loads make three yards of bed after enough of the long litter has been shaken out for covering the bed. The price paid is high, but to obtain good manure suitable for the purpose it has to be paid for accordingly; it might no doubt be had cheaper by contract. But hitherto I have not included a horse and cart as portions of my stock in trade, but have always hired. The man whom I employ understands the quality of manure that is needed, and he devotes his whole time to collecting it from the London stables during the Mushroom-growing season. After the beds are exhausted the decayed manure usually sells readily at 1s. 3d. per yard of bed, or 2s. 6d. per load. Those having experience of manure say that no kind is better suited than this for enriching the soil in the London parks, squares, and gardens generally; it is also, as most gardeners know, excellent for mixing with soil for potting purposes. I have a little more than an acre of land, for which I pay £12 per year; but hitherto only about half of it has been covered with Mushroom beds, a portion of the rest being used for spawn-making. The beds, however, increase in number every year, and before the present season expires I shall gather at the least five tons of Mushrooms, against a little over two tons last year. I send them all to Covent Garden Market, where they are disposed of in the usual manner by a salesman. They are sorted into three different sizes, and are all packed in chip punnets, each containing a pound. They have this autumn fetched higher prices than I ever knew at the same season of the year. The small buttons have been making 2s. per lb., and the larger Mushrooms 1s. 6d., and the season promises to be one of the best in my experience. I should like for farmers, and indeed all who keep horses, also gardeners and even cottagers, to be made acquainted with this system of Mushroom culture, as they might benefit themselves considerably. At present there is practically no supply around large provincial cities and towns, in which the prices for Mushrooms usually rule about 6d. per lb. higher than in London, from whence they have to be obtained. I am not a gardener, but a carpenter by trade. I had a relative who many years ago grew Mushrooms in a small way, and I resolved to endeavour to improve on the plan I had seen, and reduce Mushroom-growing to a system by which I might obtain a livelihood. I am glad to say that by perseverance I have succeeded, and now I no more think of a failure when I plant the spawn than a gardener does when he plants his Potatoes and sows his Peas."

The above letter is adduced as affording conclusive evidence of the remunerative character of Mushrooms when their culture is intelligently pursued and a sound practice well carried out. Here is an instance with manure costly, rent high, labour expensive—£4 being paid to three men weekly—or four families being supported off less than an acre of ground at the rent above named. Could similar results be achieved by the culture of any other outdoor crops of fruits or vegetables? If so, what are they? We now go a step further in anticipation of the question which naturally arises relative to the

COST AND VALUE OF AN ACRE OF MUSHROOMS.

Remembering that the entire cost of each lineal yard of bed is 5s., and the value of the produce therefrom 15s., we have only to ascertain the length of beds that can be placed on an acre to arrive at their total cost and value. The beds, as has been stated, are $2\frac{1}{2}$ feet in width; but for accommodating the litter that is used for covering them, and for purposes of gathering, space has to be reserved between the beds. Allowing a width of 5 feet between each two beds, which is more than sufficient, it will be perceived that the beds will actually occupy one-third of the ground, two-thirds being reserved for working purposes, so that practically the width devoted to each bed is $7\frac{1}{2}$ feet, or $2\frac{1}{2}$ yards. There being 4840 square yards in an acre, that space will hold a length of 1936 lineal yards of beds $2\frac{1}{2}$ feet wide, with 5 feet spaces between the beds. The issue is now simple.

	£	s.	d.
1936 lineal yards, at 15s. per yard	1452	0	0
Total cost of production, 5s. per yard...............	484	0	0
Balance	968	0	0
Deduct rent per acre.............................£12 ⎱	18	0	0
Also half an acre for preparing manure ... 6 ⎰			
Actual profit	950	0	0

It must be added, however, that while to Mr. Barter the total cost of production is only 5s. a yard (the making of Mushroom spawn being included in the labour account), yet purchasers of spawn would incur a further cost of 1s. per yard, or £96 16s. per acre, and thus the actual profit would be reduced to £853 4s., for an acre of Mushrooms.

However remarkable, even apparently sensational, the above sum may appear, it is believed to be in no manner exaggerated. In order, however, to check the accuracy of the figures, Mr. Barter, in total ignorance of the amount per acre that had been thus ascertained, was requested to extract from his books the quantities of Mushrooms sold monthly during one entire season, with the extent of beds from which they were gathered. He obligingly complied, and the following is the return submitted, its accuracy being guaranteed by the culti-vator. It will be seen that the only two months in which there were no returns are August and September, the latter being the Mushroom month in the open air. The season of cultivated Mushrooms thus commences in October and ends in July.

MUSHROOMS SOLD MONTHLY FROM 500 LINEAL YARDS OF BEDS.

	lbs.
October	362
November	460
December	1142
January	768
February	652
March	707
April	1283
May	1031
June	686
July	265
	7356

The above quantity was actually sent to market off a length of 500 yards of beds, and sold for £367 16s.: add to the total at least 50 lbs. disposed of at home for £2 10s., and further add 200 lbs. made into ketchup, for which the actual value is 6d. per lb., and we find the gross value of the produce £375 6s. from slightly over a quarter of an acre of land. Multiply the amount by 4, and we have £1501 4s. against the above estimate of £1452, which is, therefore, submitted as fair, and certainly not excessive. As further evidence that Mushrooms can be grown outdoors with some approach to regularity, and that a good crop is not a matter of chance, a record of the yield from 150 yards of beds during one month—April, 1882—may be adduced. The following are the dates of gathering and the quantities sold :—April 1st, 122 lbs. ; 4th, 73 lbs. ; 6th, 114 lbs. ; 8th, 108 lbs.; 11th, 160 lbs.; 13th, 104 lbs.; 15th, 159 lbs. ; 18th, 207 lbs. ; 20th, 180 lbs. ; 22nd, 180 lbs. ; 25th, 150 lbs. ; 27th, 222 lbs.; 29th, 221 lbs.; or a total of 2000 lbs. This is a perfectly fair example of ordinary practice. It may also be stated that one bed 25 yards long yielded in the same month 529 lbs. during three weeks—namely, 159 lbs. one week, 180 lbs. the next, and 170 lbs. the last week of the month. Here, then, is a great field for cultivators ; so great is it, and so tempting must it be to those who possess manure and land to enter on Mushroom culture on a large scale, that it is prudent to point out a possible source of danger to those who are inexperienced in the work.

ANOTHER WORD OF CAUTION.

Evidence having been adduced in support of the statement that no vegetable nor fruit crop will give equal returns to the cultivator of a given plot of ground that Mushrooms will when cultivated intelligently and well, it becomes necessary to point out the inadvisability of those who have had no experience whatever in the cultivation of this crop entering on the practice on a large scale at the first. This, as has been shown, would involve a considerable outlay, and there is always a risk of failure following the first essay in a new undertaking. Although the details of culture will be stated as plainly as possible, and without the slightest reservation on any point that may contribute to success, yet a little experience is requisite for the whole matter to be appreciated. A few "object lessons" are essential, and fortunately these may with slight risk and outlay be easily provided by at least a hundred thousand people in this country who have at their command every necessary for that purpose.

In Mushroom-growing a safe principle to be acted

upon is for many to commence on a small scale at first,
rather than a few to attempt the work on a large scale;
then if the first effort should not be successful little
will have been lost, while valuable experience will have
been gained. Instead of one man who is inexperienced
in the work purchasing manure largely and incurring
much expense in labour by making half a mile of beds,
let the thousands of those who have manure make beds
from 5 to 10 yards in length as an experiment. The
little labour requisite for this will not be missed; and
even should the beds prove barren, and there is no
reason that they should, the material can still be used
for enriching the land. This is the system that the
above - mentioned successful cultivator adopted, and
that has also been pursued by market gardeners in the
neighbourhood of London, with whom Mushrooms form
one of the most remunerative crops. Why should not
other large cities and towns be similarly well supplied,
such as Liverpool, Manchester, Birmingham, Leeds,
Bradford, Sheffield, Bristol, Newcastle, Edinburgh,
Glasgow, Dublin, Belfast, and numberless others from
the districts surrounding them where horses are plentiful, space and soil abundant, and labour as cheap as
near the metropolis? There is no valid reason that
every district should not afford a full supply of this
esculent for the requirements of the inhabitants in that
district, instead of, as is the case at present, at least
ten millions of people being practically dependent on
growers near the metropolis, and imported produce in
the form of thousands of pounds of tinned Mushrooms
that are sold by grocers and others in all parts of the
kingdom. Indeed, there is no substantial obstacle
against the establishment of an important industry and,
as suggested by Mr. Thomas, our having a surplus of
produce for export purposes. Mushrooms grown in the
open air in England are superior both in size and quality
to those grown in caves in France, and they can be
grown at less cost by our system than by theirs. There
is thus every encouragement for a great number of persons to attempt their culture on a small scale, with a
determination to become competent, and what may be
termed self-made Mushroom growers. There are

" self-taught " individuals in every craft and calling, and not a few of these have become masters in their vocation, but their competency was not attained without effort and without reverses. He who faints at failures is not likely to rise above mediocrity, if he reaches it. It has been said of Carey, the cobbler missionary, by whose unceasing labour the Bible was translated into sixteen languages, that after being, when a boy, confined to his bed for many weeks in consequence of a fall from a tree he had determined to climb, the first thing he did on recovering his strength was to " go and climb that tree." It is this spirit that should animate all who are engaged in any worthy occupation, and it is certain if they enjoy the blessing of health that they will sooner or later succeed in their object.

INFORMATION WANTED.

It is gratifying to observe that there is a laudable desire on the part of those connected, however intimately or remotely, with the cultivation of the soil, to impart information that shall be useful. Everyone, from the most exalted and greatest landed proprietors down and through the various grades of society—clergymen, scientific men, professional men, literary men, farmers, gardeners, and cottagers—all are most ready in their endeavour to increase the productiveness of the land. The great body of consumers in towns now perceive that they also share in the advantages of a bountiful soil, and the producers of food are equally ready to admit that a thrifty population is at the root of their prosperity.

" Information wanted " is the motto of the times ; it is wanted on everything by which materials of whatever kind can be converted into money. That instruction is wanted, or needed, on a simple and profitable system of turning manure into money through the agency of Mush-rooms, is apparent from the fact that even the great majority of gardeners are practically unacquainted with the method that will be described. This is no fault of theirs, for they cannot be expected to know what they have never been taught ; and it were as unreasonable to expect them to become proficient at the first attempt as it would be to expect a carpenter to make a pianoforte, or a blacksmith to construct a locomotive, without some experience in his work. It is, however, fair to expect that those who have had no opportunities for practising the particular work under notice, nor seen it successfully carried out, will no longer assert that the system is impracticable in the face of results that have been adduced, and which it is not possible to explain away. Given the proper materials for growing Mushrooms in the open air, every intelligent cultivator who is under the impression that the work cannot be done, can, if he is earnestly desirous, do it, and by a little patient endeavour he may enjoy the singular pleasure of being surprised at his own success.

CHIEF ESSENTIALS FOR GROWING MUSHROOMS.

THESE are mainly five. 1, a supply of manure from horse stables; 2, good spawn; 3, equable and moderate temperature and moisture; 4, fertile soil; 5, intelligent supervision. The mere narration of the chief requisites is, however, not sufficient for the information of the inexperienced, and details founded on successful practice are indispensable. In order that the information now sought to be imparted may be of substantial use, the following remarks will be plain, the chief aim and object being to induce those having the means at their disposal, but who have never given thought to the subject, to become Mushroom-growers in order that they may add usefully to their resources, and give the populations of cities and towns what they do not now possess—a good supply at a moderate cost of this most agreeable product of the farm and the garden.

MANURE FOR MUSHROOM BEDS.

As above observed this must consist mainly, and it may consist entirely, of the manure from horse stables. Other matter can be added without injury to the beds, and occasionally an admixture of Oak and Beech leaves, a slight sprinkling of tan, and even of salt and guano, have been found advantageous by some cultivators; but the three last-named ingredients must be used in a very homœpathic manner. Such tree leaves as those mentioned may, if needed, form one-third of the bulk when manure is scarce; indeed, excellent Mushrooms have been grown in beds half composed of Oak leaves, which, with manure, produce a steady and lasting heat, as the fibre they contain causes them to decay slowly. On the contrary, such large and soft leaves as Sycamore, Horse Chestnuts, and Planes are not suitable, nor are those of Elms and Poplars, as they speedily decay, and the heat which they generate quickly and violently is as suddenly dispersed, and extreme cold follows. Sudden transitions of temperature in the soil are more or less injurious to all plants, and injury is especially apparent in Mushroom culture when the mycelium is spreading through beds which are alternately too hot and too cold. Tan can only be added with benefit when the fermentation of the manure is too slow, and even then a pound or two to a barrowload will usually be sufficient. Guano and salt in mixture have the same effect, but in a greater degree, in advancing fermentation, and an ounce of each to a barrowful of the material will be ample. When the manure is somewhat poor—that is, contains a greater bulk of straw than is desirable, this very slight sprinkling of salt and guano enriches the bed and benefits the Mushrooms, and it also adds greatly to the value of the old beds for manurial purposes. But the succesful grower, whose practice will be embodied in these notes, uses none of these ingredients, except, perhaps, very occasionally a little tan. Leaves are not plentiful in London, and further, manure can be had by purchase from horses fed on hard food—that is, good corn and hay, as, for obvious reasons, it is not the custom to turn horses out to grass in the metropolis.

UNSUITABLE MANURE.

There is sufficient choice near large towns to refuse manure from those stables where the grooms are addicted to giving horses much medicine. Manure thus produced is fatal to Mushrooms, and is without doubt one cause of the failures which now and then occur in private gardens, and the origin of which cannot always be traced at the time. Neither is the manure good for the purpose in question from those stables in which Carrots are largely consumed. Thus it is conceivable, indeed it is certain, that the gardener has not unfrequently had to bear the opprobrium of failure in the Mushroom house when the real cause of that failure was in the stable. This is one of those unfortunate cases where a man is not the keeper of his own reputation. Manure, therefore, must be had, wherever this is possible, only from those stables where the horses are fed chiefly or entirely on sound hard food, as Carrots, grass, and medicine given to the animals as a system mean blank Mushroom beds ; and certainly no man should be accused of his inability to grow Mushrooms until he has failed to produce them by the use of manure of the proper kind. This being provided in sufficient quantity they can be grown if needed in the depth of winter in the middle of a field, but with a medium that is poisonous to them the most costly structure cannot avail to prevent barren beds. With manure of the character above recommended neither leaves, soil, nor any other ingredient is needed for mixing with it ; but the condition as well as the nature of the material is highly important, and this phase of the subject demands special consideration.

PREPARING THE MANURE.

The foregoing remarks apply equally to manure for growing Mushrooms on a small scale in houses and for producing them in large quantities in the open air for market purposes. Those engaged in this latter work are few, far too few, in number, and they ought to increase in the environs of towns and in those country districts that are traversed by railways, and where stations are not far distant for receiving the produce for transit to those great centres of population where Mushrooms are ever in demand. Our remarks on preparing the manure will refer more particularly to that class of cultivators who almost exclusively must prepare the material in the open air. This proper condition of the manure is a matter of the greatest moment, and next to securing good spawn is the chief essential in the production of Mushrooms. Without good spawn profitable beds cannot be had, however suitable the manure may be ; and on the other hand, even if the spawn is of the highest quality, unless the manure is of the right kind and in a proper state of decomposition for affording the requisite temperature

and moisture, the mycelium cannot permeate the mass
and the spawn will be wasted. It is not easy to determine whether inferior spawn or unsuitable manure has
been the most fertile source of failurés in Mushroom-
growing. It is satisfactory, however, to know that
good spawn is plentiful, and the preparation of the
manure not difficult. It is, in fact, much more easy to
do the work properly than to describe it in a manner
that will be intelligible to those who have no practical
knowledge on the subject. But even such individuals
possess one advantage—they have nothing to unlearn ;
and on the same principle that a tailor is preferred to a
jockey for conversion into a cavalry soldier, so we may
hope there are many persons who have never seen a
Mushroom bed made who will equal if not surpass as
cultivators those who have had considerable experience
in doing the work wrongly.

A WORD TO THE INEXPERIENCED.

For the encouragement of the uninitiated it may be
stated that one of the most successful Mushroom-
growers in England is by trade a joiner, and did not
relinquish his calling until he had been for some years a
journeyman. The question now arises—If a man who
has been trained as an artisan has by intelligent industry
and perseverance established his fame, and it is hoped is
making his fortune, by Mushroom-growing, cannot
hundreds of others, even on a comparatively small
scale, make themselves proficient in the same work ?
Unquestionably they can if they will follow instructions intelligently and apply themselves with diligence
towards acquiring competency in an occupation that
is at once interesting and in a remarkable degree
profitable.

In the sketch of a mushroom ground previously given
the beds are covered ; in the figure on the opposite page
a portion of a bed is represented from which the crop
is being gathered. It is not an ideal figure, but is
"taken from life." So far from the engraving being
exaggerated, strict accuracy compels the observation
that on some other portions of the bed the crop was

much heavier ; indeed, the Mushrooms were crowded so densely as to admirably represent, in the struggle for development, the working of the celebrated Darwinian doctrine of the "Survival of the Fittest."

PREPARING THE MANURE—FAULTY METHODS.

In preparing manure for Mushroom beds, two what may be termed extreme practices have been more or less generally advocated, and one of them has been exten-

Outdoor Mushroom Bed.

sively adopted. These practices will be mentioned in order that they may be avoided, for both are faulty. The first and very common plan is to gather horse droppings from the stables daily, excluding all straw from them. By this mode, if there are few horses, a considerable times elapses before sufficient material is obtained for a bed. In the meantime the droppings are spread as thinly as possible in a shed, and at least a portion of them become so dry that there is little virtue left in them ; and even if the mycelium spreads through the beds, the resulting crops are light, the Mushrooms

small, and the gatherings few. On this old exhaustive
process of preparing the manure, Mr. Gilbert of
Burghley, a most successful grower of Mushrooms both
in houses and in the open air, remarks with great force,
" To gather horse droppings, then lay them in a shed,
dry them and turn them till there is no strength left in
them, and then to expect Mushrooms, is to me something
like madness." If, on the other hand, droppings are
plentiful and enough is gathered in a short time for use,
the material after sundry turnings is formed into a bed.
In the majority of cases the heat is generated quickly
and violently, and very frequently holes are made all over
the bed with a dibber to reduce the temperature, which
holes also serve as receptacles for lumps of spawn
when the heat has subsided. This is not a sound mode
of procedure, and if productive and long-lasting beds
follow it is more the result of chance than of good
management. The only really satisfactory reflection in
connection with such beds is that it is somewhat
difficult to prevent Mushrooms growing when good
spawn is plentiful, and therefore, when similar spawn is
placed in a suitable medium, good crops are easily produced.

The last-named system is unsound in two respects.
First, it is in the nature of fermenting materials that
heat quickly and violently to cool rapidly and suddenly,
the inevitable result being that the bed is at first far too
hot, and the means taken to cool it deprives it of its
virtues—ammonia—and it is afterwards too cold for the
requirements of the crop, and the Mushroom supply, if
a supply follows, is necessarily of short duration.
Secondly, when spawn is inserted in a smooth hole made
with a dibber, and consequently tapering to a point, it is
impossible that an angular substance can completely
occupy the space that has been thus provided. There
must at least be a cavity below the spawn, and there
vapour, not always sweet, accumulates and prevents the
growth of the mycelium. Much experience has shown
that cultivators have too often to depend on weak and
inferior spawn, but the same experience has also shown
conclusively that much good spawn has been spoiled by
the practice indicated. This ancient, tedious, and

elaborate mode of collecting and preparing the manure is wrong in principle. Still it may be urged that many good Mushroom beds have resulted from it. No doubt this is so, but failures have been still more numerous, and any practice that produces more blanks than prizes is essentially faulty. The evils of overheating incident to the above process have been frequently mitigated, and sometimes averted, by mixing soil with the manure, and other methods that are known to culti- vators; but it is not for these—the few—that these remarks are intended, but for the far greater number— those on the one hand who know a little about the subject of Mushroom culture but not enough for insur- ing good beds always, and on the other that still greater body who know nothing about the practice, yet who have the means at disposal, and only need the skill for producing crops of great value. The object is to afford sound guidance for these by first stating errors that they may be avoided, and then submitting instructions as plainly and clearly as possible, that they may be followed with a fair prospect if not an absolute assur- ance of success accruing.

UNPURIFIED MANURE.

The next practice for avoidance is what may be termed the rough-and-ready one of first placing the manure, short straw and droppings, in a heap to heat, and when fermentation is brisk turning it over once or twice at the most, and then forming it into beds. Even if good crops of Mushrooms have followed, the practice is, notwithstanding, unsafe, and the material must have been specially sweet to begin with by previous fermen- tation and disturbance. The mycelium of the fungus will not permeate an impure medium. No plant re- quires purer and sweeter fare than the Mushroom does. Some other kinds of fungi will luxuriate in the most offensive matter, indeed such is essential to them, but this is certainly not one of them. If the manure of which a bed is made is in the slightest degree repulsive to the operator it will undoubtedly prove detrimental to the crop he is hoping to secure. So dainty is the Mush-

room that it selects the healthiest, sweetest pastures for
its home, and even soil that contains fresh manure is
unsuitable for surfacing the beds. Avoid, then, on the
one hand the old over-dried straw-excluding dropping-
system, and on the other the use of rank materials
resulting from insufficient turning and sweetening, and
over-haste in making up the beds.

CORRECT PRACTICES.

Having submitted systems that should be avoided,
endeavour shall now be made to detail the method
that should be adopted in preparing manure for Mushrooms. Bearing in mind that the manure must be
procured from those stables where the horses are fed
chiefly or entirely with hard dry food, let it be prepared as follows—the object being the formation of beds
either in the open air or in houses. Let the manure
be gathered precisely as the grooms remove it from the
stalls. By far the greater bulk of it will be straw more
or less stained; still, exclude none of this straw, for any
portion of it that may not be wanted for fermentation
will serve a very important purpose. On the arrival of
the stable refuse at the preparing ground let it be
forked over, casting aside the long and comparatively
clean straw only, such as in itself will generate but
little heat if placed in a moderate-sized heap; the remainder, which may consist of from one-half straw and
one-half droppings to two-thirds of the former and one-
third of the latter, to be mixed and formed into a heap
as if building a hotbed for a frame. It will seldom be
necessary to water it, except perhaps when prepared in
August, or early September, and in very dry weather in
spring; still if water is needed to accelerate decomposition apply it. In the course of from four to six
days, according to the nature of the manure and the
weather, fermentation will be active and the mass hot.
The work of turning and purifying must now commence, the former to be carefully done or the latter
will not be effected. Every lock of straw and flake of
manure which adheres together must be separated, the
whole being thoroughly incorporated, the outside por-

tions of the heap being placed in the centre. For the purpose of making the lower part of an ordinary hot-bed, one turning after this will often suffice ; but it will seldom indeed suffice for a Mushroom bed, first because the material would not be sweet enough, and secondly because decomposition would not be sufficiently advanced. For insuring both these conditions, which are important, from four to six turnings on alternate days are necessary. By this practice the mass is sweetened and the straw broken and partially decayed with the least possible loss of ammonia. The object should be to retain as much of this as possible consistently with the dissipation of other gases that are obnoxious alike to man and to Mushrooms. It should be observed that when much straw is decomposed with the droppings tree leaves are not needed, and are only of real service when straw is excluded.

THE CONDITION OF THE MATERIALS.

The right condition of the mass for making up in the beds can only be determined by its appearance and by the sense of smell. It is possible that a heap of manure may be sweet and yet not be quite sufficiently decomposed for our purpose, and on the other hand it may be in a proper state of decay and yet not be sweet ; but usually, if the work of turning and mixing is done with care and intelligence, purity and texture will be synchronous ; both conditions will be attained at once, and the mass will be ready for use. As the manure and its preparation constitute the very foundation for success in Mushroom culture it is necessary to bestow careful attention on this matter. Persons having experience in heating with fermenting materials can without difficulty determine when the mass can be safely used ; but it is certain that all who attempt to grow Mushrooms do not always employ the best medium for the purpose. They either reject too much straw, a frequent occurrence, or when they include it in the mass they make the beds too soon—that is, before the requisite degree of decomposition has been attained. It may be stated for the benefit of the inexperienced as

nearly as possible the condition the material should be
in for the purpose in question. In appearance there
should be a homogeneous or inseparable mass of straw
and droppings, the former preponderating, and broken
in particles, none of which should exceed 9 inches, and
few 6 inches in length, the majority being shorter ; the
mass should have a slightly greasy appearance, be warm
brown in colour, and more than " warm " as regards
temperature—in fact it should be as hot as the hand
can be borne in it. And now to the test for purity.
This is simple. Draw a large handful from the interior
of the bulk and apply it to the nostrils ; if the result is
in any degree offensive another turning is needful, but
if no impurity is detected then the mass may be regarded as sweet. That is a negative test. A positive
test is this—a rather pungent and somewhat agreeable
scent having a suspicion of the odour of Mushrooms.
When this is the result we have the most tangible
evidence of possessing a medium in the best manner
suited for the production of Mushrooms. There is yet
another element that must not be overlooked—namely,
that of moisture. If the mass is too wet its decay will
be too rapid ; if it is too dry a steady and continuous
heat will not be maintained. Generally speaking,
however, when a heap of fermenting manure is well
managed the four important requisites—texture, heat,
purity, and moisture, will be present in the proper
relative proportions ; but still, with the object of making
that matter plain to all, it may be said that the material
must be sufficiently moist to be pressed into a firm
adherent mass, yet not so wet that a drop of water can
be squeezed from a handful of it by the greatest mus-
cular pressure. As clearly as possible the various tests
have been submitted, in order that the uninitiated may
be able to start on a firm and sound basis, with good
hope of deriving profitable returns sooner or later in
Mushroom culture. But for achieving success every
detail must be carried out thoughtfully. The brain
must guide the hand in everything, for, as Lord Bacon
has forcibly recorded, "Neither the naked hand nor
the understanding, left to itself, can do much ; the
work is accomplished by instruments and helps, of

which the need is not less for the understanding than the hand."

SITE FOR MUSHROOM BEDS.

Wherever the site and soil are such that water does not accumulate on the surface, there the beds may be arranged and Mushrooms grown. But shelter from cold penetrating winds is a decided advantage. Mr. Barter's Mushroom ground is fully exposed to the north and east, yet with the aid of wattled hurdles he achieves the results that have been recorded. Mr. Gilbert's beds, though nearly a hundred miles further north, are much more favourably situated. They are arranged in a strip of ground about 100 yards long from east to west and 20 yards wide. The northern boundary is a lofty garden wall, a hedge running along the south side of the enclosure. A lean-to bed is formed along the wall facing south, the remainder of the ground being covered with ridges across the strip, and consequently at right angles with the wall. This is an admirable position, and prodigious crops are gathered; and there is no doubt whatever that if the same cultivator practised two hundred miles still further north and had a similar position he would with good manure and spawn have equally productive ridges. Shelter, then, is desirable but not essential, and there are sheltered nooks in almost every garden and homestead that could be more profitably occupied with Mushrooms than by any other crop that could be produced on the ground. If there are no such favoured places make the beds in the open the same as is done in the vegetable fields round London, and protect them sufficiently with straw and hurdles, and an ample return will be derived from the labour and material thus invested. It is important to remember that if the soil is good on the site the beds are to occupy, it should be previously removed to a depth of several inches and placed in a heap, as it can be far more profitably employed on the beds than under them. The excavations so formed can be filled with rubble, thus providing dry foundations for the beds.

SIZE OF THE BEDS.

The size of beds or ridges for the culture of Mushrooms in the open air should, as before mentioned, be
2½ feet wide at the base, about 6 inches wide at the
top, and 2½ feet high. At the angle thus formed soil
will adhere to the sides firmly, while a great portion of
rain will pass off freely, especially if the top is slightly
rounded, as it should be, not quite flat. If the angle
were less acute the beds might be saturated during
heavy falls of rain; but this does not occur when
properly made of the form described, well cased with
soil, and, if needed, protected with canvas or other suitable coverings over the straw. When this method of
Mushroom culture is adopted such covers should be in
readiness, as they will be specially needed in districts
where the rainfall is heavy, and they are also of great
service for conserving the heat of the beds during severe
weather. Beds of the form indicated also possess
another enormous advantage, especially near towns
where land is scarce and consequently dear—viz., they
just double the cultivable surface of the ground, for
while the width of the ground actually covered with
manure is only 2½ feet, the two sloping sides of each
bed of the height named obviously present a surface of
5 feet; or to show the increase of surface more fully,
suppose an acre is occupied with beds of an aggregate
length of 1936 yards and of the width stated, they
would only cover 1613 square yards, while at the same
time they afford a surface for Mushroom-production of
3226 yards without including the 6-inch space at the
top of the beds. Thus we have an exception to the old
axiom relative to the "increase of the population while
the land remains stationary." It is certainly not
" stationary " when devoted to this system of Mushroom-
culture, for, instead of the normal surface per acre of
4840 yards, we produce and utilise a surface of 6453
square yards. It is owing to this fact in a great measure
that the value of an acre of Mushrooms becomes so
extraordinary.

It is not suggested that good crops of Mushrooms

cannot be had from larger beds than above indicated. Great quantities are grown on beds ranging from 3 to 4 feet wide at the base and correspondingly high ; but beyond all doubt beds of the first-named dimensions properly made of suitable material contain all the essentials for an abundant supply of Mushrooms ; and when manure has to be purchased these comparatively small ridges have been proved to be the more economical and profitable. If the manure is of inferior quality and ot of a nature to produce and retain much heat, then larger beds are advisable, but with good manure properly prepared the ridges above recommended are sufficiently large for producing heavy crops of Mushrooms during the winter near London. In the north, and especially when manure is abundant, larger beds may be advisable; indeed they are employed with remarkable success at Burghley. The size of the ridges for certain positions and under varying conditions can soon be determined by those who earnestly attempt this, the simplest and best of all methods of Mushroom culture. But whatever the size of the beds may be, let the sides be as steep as possible, firm and smooth. It is by making the ridges too flat and loose, admitting the rain, that many failures have occurred, and thus a system has been condemned when the operators and not the system have been really at fault.

MAKING THE BEDS.

In building a bed for the first time the workman would probably find a few guide sticks useful. If he has two a yard long each, inserts them $2\frac{1}{2}$ feet apart and just 6 inches deep, draws the tops within 6 inches of each other, he has an outline section of the bed. A few sticks thus arranged at intervals would form a sure guide. He would, however, quickly learn to dispense with them, and only need a line stretched along one side to work by, the manure being wheeled on the other, which is made straight without difficulty, the eye being the sole guide, as a line, as will be apparent, could not be kept clear, The work of building should be done quickly, yet well, the material being thoroughly

shaken out during the process and pressed together
very firmly. In addition to its being heavily beaten
with forks it should also be trodden down at the least
twice, once when a depth of about 18 inches has been
packed together, and again when the ridge is 3 feet
high ; this will bring it down to 2 feet, the remaining
6 inches being made firm with the fork. The sides
must be also beaten quite firm, and then dressed or
combed down. When finished they will resemble a

Mushroom bed.

closely thatched roof in miniature, and like the roof
will throw off the rain. This is important, and the
necessity is now seen for having a good proportion of
decayed straw ; beds made wholly of the orthodox horse
droppings would inevitably be saturated and spoiled.

A bed made as described is, when finished, a work
of art, at least so a good workman would regard it.
An example is represented in the figure of a well-made
bed, which, as will be seen, is perfectly straight and
clear in outline. Such a ridge made quite firm, indeed
almost hard, is practically impervious to wet, and when

well cased with soil and covered with litter is capable of retaining sufficient heat for the growth of the mycelium and the support of a heavy crop of Mushrooms. The bed is shown with lumps of spawn inserted and partly cased with soil.

To prevent the bed heating too violently and drying in the centre too much, holes should be bored with an iron bar from 9 to 12 inches apart along the ridge to nearly the bottom of the bed, and a few sticks should be left in the bed to test the heat at any time. If the bed is made as firm as it ought to be, sticks cannot well be driven down, hence the use of the iron rods, th necessity for which indicates clearly that the ridges should when finished be very firm indeed. A few of these sticks left in the beds will on examination indicate the temperature. The ventilators are often left open for some time after the ridges have been spawned and cased ; they can be closed at any time by simply pressing in the soil.

It is not usual to finish Mushroom beds or ridges so artistically as in the example submitted ; but it is desirable that this and all work should be done in the best possible manner. The difference in cost between doing work slovenly and finishing it neatly is very slight, and the advantage in the end is in favour of the skilled workman. Unless a man in whatever he is engaged, takes pride in his work, he will never excel, and it would be greatly to our advantage as a nation if every workman would habituate himself to complete whatever he had in hand as if competing for a prize ; a higher standard of excellence would then soon be attained, and British workmen would maintain their supremacy in the competition of the world.

MUSHROOM SPAWN.

WHERE Mushrooms are largely grown, on outdoor beds especially, numbers of the larger specimens that have been left to become old and the laminæ or gills have turned almost black, the top of the Mushrooms, the pileus, will assume a brown rusted appearance. This is produced by multitudinous spores, which fall from the gills of the Mushrooms above them and are shed on the soil. But these spores never produce Mushrooms directly. They germinate under suitable conditions and produce white cobweb-like filaments, which spread

Fig. 1.   Fig. 2.

through masses of manure of the proper kind, completely permeating it, and render it mouldy or cottony in appearance by their numerous interlacings. This is the mycelium or spawn, which in a medium congenial to its growth spreads rapidly, and thickens, eventually producing tubercles which develope into Mushrooms. This briefly is the manner in which Mushrooms are propagated. In the late Mr. Smee's beautiful work, "My Garden," published by Bell and Sons, Mr. Worthington G. Smith, the eminent fungologist, has represented for the first time the spores in the act of germinating (fig. 1), and he has also shown what gardeners term a "lump of spawn," (fig. 2), or the mycelium as it is preserved and used in the culture of Mushrooms.

DISPERSION AND GERMINATION OF SPORES.

In the dispersion of the spores of Mushrooms a curious fact may be noticed, and which presumably has not been previously recorded. It is this : When a number of Mushrooms are allowed to mature on the side of a steep ridge, no matter how acute its angle may be, even if the side of the bed is almost perpendicular, all the spores will be distributed on the soil above the Mushrooms, never below them, as we might naturally expect would be the case. After a careful examination of hundreds of Mushrooms not one instance has been found where the spores fell on the ridge below, but they are always cast off in an upward direction, and frequently in such numbers as to form a snuff-like semicircle on the soil above them. Mr. Barter, with his greater opportunities for observation, states that after closely examining thousands of specimens he has never found an exception to the somewhat singular rule mentioned. But the spores do not germinate there, as the conditions are not favourable. They germinate in manure which is of a suitable character as regards its constituents, temperature, and moisture, as is the case in some cattle sheds. Many carefully conducted experiments have been made by scientific men to induce the germination of the spores by artificial means, but, while they may have succeeded, it is not known that any authenticated instances of success have been recorded.

MILLTRACK MUSHROOM SPAWN.

Mycelium was formerly plentiful in the tracks of horses which for days together in the ante-steam-driving period were engaged in a monotonous round, and forming the motive power of grinding mills and thrashing machines ; hence the term, not yet obsolete, of " milltrack" Mushroom spawn. This spawn, produced direct from the spores, is termed " virgin " spawn, and is of great strength and excellence. " Milltrack " Mushroom spawn is still offered in a few catalogues at 5s. or 6s. a bushel. The vendors, however, while probably being conscious of the possession of a good article, appear to have forgotten that milltrack spawn is practically extinct, and some of them at least are perhaps not aware that good virgin spawn is now worth two guineas a bushel, and it is only used, when it can be had, in the manufacture of spawn that is prepared in the form of bricks as used by cultivators.

FRENCH MUSHROOM SPAWN.

What is known as "French spawn," which it may be stated is by no means all made in France, is not sold in the form of bricks, but is contained in flakes of manure. Neither is it virgin spawn, nor derived immediately from it, as some persons erroneously suppose, but is spawn taken from one bed for impregnating another, and as a rule it is certainly not so strong and trustworthy as is the best spawn of English manufacture in the form of bricks. A great quantity of the so-called French spawn is made and used in some of the market gardens near London, and excellent crops of Mushrooms are produced; but in these instances it is so plentiful and there is so much choice that only the best is selected, and it is used lavishly. Its purchase in small quantities by private growers is quite another question, and they will find the spawn that is incorporated in bricks both better on the whole and more convenient. Much spawn is also imported from France and sold in boxes; and the true French spawn, it must in fairness be said, is better than that taken from old Mushroom beds in this country, inasmuch as, although practically made in the same way, it has not been weakened by a crop of Mushrooms; but as the mycelium has been produced "many removes" from the spores it is necessarily weak in comparison with the best quality sold in bricks of English manufacture. Perhaps the most conclusive evidence of the superiority of what may be termed "brick spawn" that can be adduced is the custom that prevails among some growers of Mushrooms of selling the spawn produced in their beds, and purchasing for their own use a supply of the above-named kind from the best manufacturers of it. Clever people!

MAKING "MUSHROOM BRICKS."

It were easy to describe the manufacture of Mushroom spawn in this form, for the hand that pens these lines has assisted to make numbers of bricks, but it would

Mushroom spawn shed.

not be easy to make the process intelligible to those who have no practical knowledge on the subject, and "object lessons" are requisite for the matter to be satisfactorily comprehended. Nor is the knowledge necessary for the great mass of Mushroom growers.

When a man builds a house it is of no advantage to
him to know how to make his own bricks, for he can
purchase them better and more cheaply ; so it is with
the vast majority of cultivators of Mushrooms, and
beginners especially will find it far more economical
to purchase good Mushroom spawn than to endeavour
to make it, and fail.   After a person has become competent as a Mushroom grower and contemplates cultivating the esculent on a large scale he will have gained
experience that may enable him to make his own
bricks of spawn, with little instruction from others, or
in other words he will be able to turn the information
he gains to profitable account.   This is the course
that Mr. Barter pursued.   He first grew Mushrooms
and then commenced "spawn-making" on a small
scale ; and proving equally successful in both the
demand for bricks increased, and can only now be
met by a supply of thousands of bushels annually.
The bricks, it may be stated, are 9 inches long, 6 wide,
and 2 deep, there being sixteen of these to the bushel.
There are other extensive manufacturers of Mushroom
spawn, and the supply for home and export purposes
amounts to many tons annually.   It is to the advantage
of purchasers of Mushroom spawn that the railway
charges for it are low, as it is transmitted under the
lowest scale but one—namely, manure ; indeed, the
bricks mainly consist of manure in a dried state, which
is simply the medium for preserving and conveying the
mycelium that produces the Mushrooms.   These bricks
are composed of soil and manure.   When partially dried
and in the right condition small portions of "spawn"
are inserted, and on being subjected to a genial heat the
mycelium penetrates the entire mass.   The bricks are
then packed in open sheds in a manner that permits
the air to circulate amongst them, and when kept cool
and dry the mycelium retains its strength and vitality
for years.   Some idea may be formed of the extent of
the trade in " Mushroom bricks," and of the manner in
which they are stored, on reference to the engraving on
page 39, of a portion of a shed in a Mushroom spawn
manufactory.

PREPOTENCY OF VIRGIN MUSHROOM SPAWN.

A singular circumstance remains to be noticed—namely, the prepotency of "virgin spawn," or the mycelium directly produced by the spores. It is well known that the mycelium can be transmitted from brick to brick, and may be so increased time after time, and year after year, but it is by no means well understood that it is more or less weakened by every such transmission. This probably will be "news" to a great number of readers, and in all probability it will afford the solution to some of a difficult problem. There are not many gardeners who have been long engaged in Mushroom culture who have not been perplexed now and then by the comparative failure of a bed. The materials and management were the same as before, and the bricks employed appeared good and were beyond doubt permeated by the mycelium, yet the crops resulting were unsatisfactory, the produce either being small or the beds soon exhausted, or both. It probably never occurred to the cultivators to inquire how far the mycelium had been weakened by inherent exhaustion consequent on a course of unintermittent propagation. This is a very interesting and important question. It is found in practice that to insure "strong" mycelium capable of producing the heaviest crops of the finest Mushrooms we must go to the original source and procure it as nearly as possible direct from the spores. Nor is it surprising that this should be so ; indeed it would be more surprising were it otherwise. Given equal conditions for culture, seedling plants of all kinds are stronger than those raised from portions of pre-existing-plants ; and further, it will not be disputed that excessive forcing and propagation may result in the degeneration of a species or variety of phænerogamic plants. Indeed if it were not so the old axiom would not have been established that a "strong plant cannot be made from a weak cutting." The same principle applies with at least equal force to the cryptograms ; and therefore reasoning by induction alone we have no right to expect strong Mushrooms from weak mycelium. But induction and physiology aside, we have the evidence of facts in support of the proposition in question, and experience teaches that this aspect of Mushroom culture cannot with impunity be ignored. Mr. Barter is careful never to use spawn or mycelium of more than two generations from the spores—that is to say, he finds it to his advantage to give a guinea for a small portion of virgin spawn not equal in bulk to half a crown's worth of the manufactured article for the purpose of impregnating a few bricks. It is from these bricks—the first remove—that the stock is raised that he himself uses and sells, bricks made for those who insist on a " cheap " article being permeated with mycelium a generation or more older, and consequently weaker. It will produce Mushrooms, and under favourable conditions good crops, but not such profitable beds and splendid produce as he never fails to obtain, and which he knows by experience it is impossible to obtain from weak second-class spawn that never ought to be distributed. Every gardener and every Mushroom grower ought to have no more difficulty in procuring " bricks " of the first quality than they have in obtaining new and good vegetable and flower seeds.

As pertaining to this aspect of Mushroom culture, numbers of persons cannot fail to have noticed how fat and fleshy those Mushrooms are that spring up spontaneously from decaying hotbeds in which no spawn was inserted, and they have been at a loss to understand the cause of the excellence of the produce. The chief reason is because they have been produced from mycelium direct from the spores, aided by steady growth under the influence of low temperature in the autumn.

GOOD *V.* BAD MUSHROOM SPAWN.

Until the importance of the above facts are recognised, and until good spawn is generally known by its appearance, mistakes will continue to be made in the purchase of " bricks," both by vendors of spawn and growers of Mushrooms. Extremely vague and divergent ideas obtain relative to what indicates high quality in this article. The general opinion is that the mycelium should not be apparent in the form of interlacing lines permeating the medium in which they are conveyed; but a more or less clouded mass of a mouldy nature is regarded as the best evidence of good quality. It is very easy to err in this matter. A brick may be a mass of mouldiness and yet be quite worthless; and if the mould has a spotted appearance, as if fine white sand has been dredged on and through the mass, it is certain there is no Mushroom-growing power there, and by far the best mode of treating such a brick is to throw it away. A good Mushroom brick when broken resembles a mass of silvery cobwebs. If on the outside some lines are as stout in texture as white cotton that is no proof that the brick is inferior. This external thickening of the mycelium is very frequently the result of the bricks having been closely packed on each other in a damp place, and the very growth of the filaments in reality affords evidence of the potency and strength of the spawn. If such thick threads pass entirely through the mass, and especially if there are signs of the formation of miniature tubercles, then the spawn may be regarded as " too far gone," not otherwise. It is not easy to make this matter plain, but the mycelium should be clearly and distinctly visible in lines—a confused indefinable mass of mould being unsatisfactory, as indicating weakness, and clusters of white specks being dangerous, as they denote nothing more nor less than sterility and death—but the lines should be sharply defined, as fine as the finest hair, and as pure and bright as the hoar frost on the window pane. In that condition the spawn is good, and if kept perfectly dry and cool will, as before observed, remain good and strong for many years.

INSERTING THE SPAWN.

It is worthy of special notice that those who are extensively and successfully engaged in growing Mushrooms for market, not only find it to their advantage to use spawn liberally but to insert it in large lumps.

It is found the best practice to divide a brick into eight portions, and insert these about 9 inches apart, the smooth sides being placed outwards, and level or nearly so with the surface of the ridges. When the work is done those portions are plainly visible and are well represented in the engraving on page 34. No holes are made for receiving the lumps, but the manure is simply held up with the left hand, and they are forcibly pressed in with the right. There are then no interstices between the spawn and manure for the accumulation of steam, which if allowed destroys the mycelium. The reason why small portions of the spawn bricks are not deemed safe is this—if the bed should happen to be a little too hot or too wet it might injure if not kill the mycelium on the outside of the lumps, and if these were small the danger of the whole being destroyed would be great, but being large the risk of this occurring is reduced to a minimum, as if the outsides of the lumps were damaged, the mycelium in the interior might be as safe and good as ever. The wisdom and even economy of using large pieces will now be apparent. There is scarcely any doubt that numbers of Mushroom beds have been rendered effete by breaking up the bricks into too many and consequently too small portions when using them. It is far better to use large pieces, even if they are inserted at wider intervals, than to use small portions and insert them much nearer together. The somewhat fanciful practice of crushing the bricks almost to powder, and spreading the particles on the surface of a bed as if sowing seed before adding the soil, cannot be recommended. It is not adopted by growers of Mushrooms for market because considered wasteful, as if it results in anything at all it is a myriad of pea-like heads that are worse than useless, as they are not only worthless but arrest the growth of finer Mushrooms from the stronger mycelium in the interior of the bed.

The time for inserting the spawn is when the heat of the bed is decreasing, but has not fallen below 80° Fahr., an inch below the surface. This proper temperature can be ascertained by placing a thermometer in the bed, but it will not be necessary to use it many times. Growers of produce for market judge of the heat by the hand, and when the manure is a little warmer than the hand is when placed amongst it the spawn is inserted. It is never safe to do this when the heat is rising, as it may afterwards increase and kill the mycelium. If the spawn is good and the bed in the right condition the former will commence spreading or "running" in three days. Then, and not till then, the bed is cased with soil. Previously, if needed, it is covered with litter of the thickness requisite for maintaining the necessary heat. After being soiled it is again covered with the same object; and it may be observed that so long as the surface of the bed under the litter is in the slightest degree warmer than the hand the temperature is right for Mushrooms.

SOIL FOR MUSHROOMS.

An opinion is somewhat widely entertained that it is of no great consequence what kind of soil is used for surfacing Mushroom beds. It is argued that the crop derives its support from the manure, not from the soil; indeed, a scientific writer has stated that soil is not necessary for Mushrooms, and he therefore did not place it on his beds from which he gathered what to him were satisfactory crops. Beyond doubt the material of which a Mushroom bed is made is of primary importance, and its character exerts a great influence on both the quantity of Mushrooms that are produced and their size. But the soil exercises an influence too, and, all other conditions being equal, the cultivator who has the command of strong turfy loam will obtain the greatest weight of produce from his beds. The material with which the Mushroom beds in the caves in France are covered is light and poor, and the Mushrooms are small. The soil which Mr. Barter uses is heavy and turfy, just such as a gardener would covet for growing Roses and Chrysanthemums, and the produce is large, Mushrooms often being cut weighing half a pound each. Thousands are gathered with stems varying from 1 to 2 inches in diameter, the pileus being an inch and upwards in thickness. "Too large," possibly some may say, especially those who only grow small ones; but those who grow Mushrooms for sale and can sell all they grow, are not afraid of growing them too large. For large Mushrooms, provided they are young, fresh, and only partially expanded, there is a great demand, especially in hotels that are patronised by foreign visitors to this country. The French may possibly prefer "buttons" at home; but it is certain they enjoy the large fat "broilers" here, and they seldom fail to ask for the fine rich juicy specimens that they can only find in England. Now to produce these, which are the most remunerative to the grower, strong and rich soil is essential—not soil recently enriched with manure, for the use of that is a mistake—but soil that is naturally fertile, such as the top spit from a pasture in which Buttercups are more plentiful than Daisies, the former indicating fertility, the latter sterility, when they are present in great numbers. There is no doubt whatever that Mushrooms derive a portion of their support from the soil with which the beds are cased. There is the same difference in the character of their roots as there is in those of other plants—in light, poor, and sandy soil they are small and numerous; in strong rich soil they are few and large, and the growth corresponds with the roots—strong when they are strong, weak when they are weak.

The fact that Mushrooms derive support from the soil, and in so doing deprive it of a portion of its constituents, is proved by the circumstance that if the soil is removed from a bed that has produced heavily, and is at once applied to a portion of a new bed, the remaining portion being cased with fresh soil, the difference in the weight of the produce from the two portions will be very apparent and overwhelmingly in favour of the fresh soil. Mr. Plant, a gardener near Manchester, has adduced conclusive evidence that Mushrooms are improved by the soil with which the beds are covered. He says in the *Journal of Horticulture*, page 193, vol. iv., third series :—" During the long frost of 1879-80 we had not sufficient material to soil a Mushroom bed, everything being frozen, so we turned a number of old Chrysanthemums out of their pots and used the soil, which had been very liberally mixed with ground bones—so much so that when spread on the bed and smoothed over it looked more like an asphalt walk than a Mushroom bed. The result was marvellous—such a crop of large fleshy Mushrooms as I never saw before." This experience is suggestive, and those who have only poor soil at their command for surfacing Mushroom beds would probably find it profitable to enrich it in the manner indicated, or add bonemeal at the rate of about a quart to a bushel of soil, and if light and sandy also a quarter of a pound of salt, the whole to be well mixed. But as above intimated, it must not be enriched with ordinary manure, or some unwelcome fungi might, and probably would, become established in the beds and do serious injury. Where soil is good for the purpose in question, yet scarce, it may be carefully removed from the beds, excluding all manurial particles, and mixed to the extent of one-half with fresh soil, turned over a few times during the season, then be used again for further crops. When ordinary garden soil is employed for Mushroom beds it is a safe practice to remove a few inches from the surface that may contain undecomposed manure, and select that immediately below it, always giving preference to strong over light soil when there is any choice in the matter ; but never under any circumstances permit any particles of manure to be mixed with the soil for surfacing Mushroom beds if troublesome, and it may be ruinous, crops of obnoxious fungi are to be averted.

CASING THE BEDS.

A section of the casing is shown in the figure previously referred to on page 34. The thickness of the soil on Mushroom beds must be governed by its nature. If very heavy it will only need to be an inch thick when beaten as firmly as possible ; if of medium texture it may be $1\frac{1}{2}$ inch thick ; if light or of a sandy nature 2 inches. When the work of casing is well done it seals up the heat in the bed to a surprising extent ; but it will not do this effectually if the orthodox plan is followed of dipping the spade in water, and plastering the soil, making it smooth as a cement floor. It should be made firm and also smooth, but the soil must be sufficiently moist for the necessary compression, and should be watered to make it so, if needed, before being placed on the beds. There is a very good reason for this which all who are engaged in growing Mushrooms, or trying to grow them, do not fully comprehend. When the surface is plastered like mortar it shrinks sooner or later and forms fissures. If these are produced quickly the heat and virtues of the bed escape through them ; if they do not form for some weeks and the soil has become permeated with the mycelium the delicate threads are broken, and when this is the case we have no more right to expect an abundance of fine Mushrooms than we have to expect that a telegraphic message will be transmitted when the wires are cut. It is this cutting off the lines of supply from the interior to the surface of the beds that is the primary cause of Mushrooms ceasing to grow after they have formed, turning brown, and withering. The shrinkage of the soil breaks these slender lines of communication, and they are not unfrequently severed by the weight of a man being suddenly thrown on the bed, that weight, as *is* common, resting on one hand for the purpose of some portion of the bed being more easily reached with the other. It is not the mere weight that does the injury, but the jerking manner in which it is applied. This may appear a small matter to dwell on, but like a number of other small matters it is of more importance than is apparent at the first glance. The withering of thousands of Mushrooms have perplexed many cultivators. The beds and house have neither been too wet nor too dry, too hot nor too cold, yet the pea-like Mushrooms have refused to move, except backwards. The snapping of the extremely brittle and cobweb-like mycelium is with much confidence submitted as the chief cause of the evil, and it is a little surprising it has not been submitted before.

TEMPERATURE FOR MUSHROOMS.

September being the month in which Mushrooms are produced the most bountifully in pastures, the temperature of that month will indicate their requirements under cultivation. It is certain that not a few failures occur in Mushroom houses by too much heat accompanied by an unduly dry atmosphere, such as is produced by hot-water pipes and a deficient supply of moisture. As a rule those houses in which Mushrooms succeed the best are kept at a temperature ranging from 55° to 60°, a genial atmosphere being at the same time maintained. Now, what do we find in the

E

open air during the Mushroom-growing month—September ? Those who will take the trouble to examine the
daily September (London) temperatures for the past ten
years and will take the means for the whole period will
find the maximum to be 67·7° and the minimum 48·8°,
or a general mean of 58·2°. How far is this from the
temperature of a well-managed Mushroom house ?
" Rather too high," perhaps some may say. Possibly
it is. Neither is the average quite fair as applied to
Mushrooms, as the figures represent the temperature
at 4 feet from the ground, and Mushrooms do not grow
there, at any rate in the open air. On the contrary,
they nestle among the much colder dew-bespangled
grass, where the mean minimum radiation temperature
of the past decade averaged only 47·1°. Now if we
ake the average between this, the lowest point, with
t he above-mentioned highest, we reduce the average by
1°—viz., 57·2°. This temperature is thus ample for
Mushrooms ; indeed, it is practically too high, as they
grow much quicker during the colder air and moister
surroundings of night than under the increased heat
and drier air of the day.   Still, were it not for the comparatively high day temperature of nearly 70°, the
earth's heat would not be retained at the requisite
degree for the crop ; and what is this ? The average
for the period named is at a foot below the surface
58·1° ; or, what is a little curious, almost identical with
the average mean of the air, 58·2°. As near, then, as
can be ascertained from the book of Nature from 55° to
58° Fahr. may be stated as the proper temperature for
Mushrooms. That they will endure more heat than
represented is unquestionable, and that they will grow
freely under a lower temperature is undeniable, for this
the minimum grass radiation figures demonstrate. And
what do these September temperatures suggest ? First,
that there is a danger of keeping Mushroom houses too
warm ; and secondly, what is more important for our
purpose, that the heat indicated can easily be maintained with a body of fermenting materials in the open
air, and straw to cover the beds and arrest radiation.
On a mild day in January of the year 1882 the
radiation temperature of a bed that was just com-

mencing bearing heavily in the open air was 60° under
a layer of 9 inches of straw. This was a little too high,
as the Mushrooms were rather drawn. On a colder day
it would have been 5° lower, and if it had been 15°
colder no harm would have been done, only the growth
of the Mushrooms would have been slower, or much
about that of those in pastures when the radiation
temperature on grass is equally low as it often is in
September.

MUSHROOMS *V.* FROST.

Cold does no real injury to Mushroom beds, it only
arrests the growth of the mycelium—does not destroy it.
During the severe weather of December, 1880, some
outdoor ridges were frozen quite through, and were
like a mass of stone, yet on the return of genial weather
the same beds produced abundant crops. This is a
very important fact, and shows that the Mushroom
is not such a tender plant as is generally imagined,
and that a failure is not likely to follow if the
heat cannot be maintained at some fancy figure.
But it must be stated that Mushrooms already formed
are liable to injury by extreme frost. It is only the
mycelium that can endure it with impunity; but this
circumstance alone is gratifying, and the experience
proves that Mushroom-growing on outdoor beds in
winter is perfectly safe. Since those notes were written
a correspondent of the *Journal of Horticulture* (page
170, vol. iv.) communicated an article containing the
following evidence bearing on this subject:—"Two
years ago last autumn I made two beds in a cold shed
with a north aspect. They were spawned and soiled in
the usual way, and then left all that severe winter. I
looked at them sometimes in passing, and found them
frozen as hard as a brick wall. I never expected to
have a Mushroom from either of them, for I had always
been taught that if a bed became frozen it would never
bear any Mushrooms. In the spring I told the men
to wheel both beds into the garden for manure, I
happened to be present when the men started, and the
first spadeful that was taken up showed that spawn had
worked all over the bed like a network. I immediately

stopped all operations and had the beds covered with litter, and they turned out two of the best beds of Mushrooms I ever saw."

That a low temperature is not fatal to the growth of Mushrooms is apparent from the fact of their presence at the base of hotbeds late in the autumn ; indeed, fine examples have been gathered which were pushing their way through a covering of snow. This no doubt was exceptional, and was without question the effect of very strong mycelium produced direct from the spores, as previously alluded to. While such low temperatures must not be sought for, it may still be asserted with much confidence that a high temperature and dry atmosphere are inimical to Mushrooms, and the cause of many failures and unsatisfactory beds.

INTELLIGENT ROUTINE.

This consists chiefly in covering the beds for maintaining an equable temperature, watering them at the proper time and in the right manner, and gathering the crops. As previously mentioned, sufficient straw can be shaken from the manure on its arrival from the stables for the purpose of covering the beds. There can be no better material than this—indeed, no other is so good for placing in immediate contact with the surface of a Mushroom bed. If during unusually severe weather clean straw or fern must be used, it should always be placed on the other covering, never on the soil under it, as it is somewhat strange to observe that when this has been done after Mushrooms have commenced growing considerable injury has resulted to the crop. The long litter shaken out from the manure is placed in a large heap and heats more or less ; it should, however, not be turned, but be allowed to heat itself dry, and it will then be in the best possible condition for use. Its peculiar nature and smell appear to be precisely suitable for Mushrooms ; at any rate they are produced far more freely under such a covering than under a layer of sweet clean straw or hay. A sufficiency of this litter should therefore be secured if possible, and it can usually be obtained if the manure is collected, long and short together, just as comes from the stables. There is a danger in gathering the manure that the long may be refused, under the impression that it will not decay sufficiently for use in the beds. It certainly will not decay to that extent, but it is of the greatest service nevertheless, for it is important to remember that, however suitable the decayed portion may be and strong the spawn, if the beds are not thickly covered with proper material satisfactory crops of Mushrooms cannot be produced.

The proper degree of thickness of the covering can

only be determined by the heat in the beds and the weather. If the weather is mild and the bed comparatively new a covering of 6 inches of litter will suffice. If the bed is old and the temperature of the air remains still mild, the covering must be twice that thickness; while during severe and prolonged frost 2 feet or more in depth of straw, protected with mats, canvas, or some such material, will be absolutely necessary, and sometimes the beds are covered 3 feet thick. Beginners, however, should endeavour to have beds to come in bearing in October or April, as Mushrooms grow with freedom then, and experience would be gained for extending the period of gathering when greater care is needed. The proper temperature of a bed can be determined by the hand. If when it is placed on the surface under the straw and the slightest possible warmth is felt, that will suffice; or, for the sake of greater accuracy, if a thermometer is laid on the soil at night, and in the morning when the straw is removed the temperature is neither many degrees below or above 50°, it will be safe. The instrument is no doubt a useful guide for the experienced, but it is certain to be dispensed with after a few crops have been gathered. Mushrooms will form and grow at a temperature of 40° when the bed is permeated with strong spawn; but their movement is slow, and a mean ranging from 10° or 15° higher should, if possible, be maintained.

WATERING MUSHROOM BEDS.

During bright weather in autumn, spring, and especially early summer, when the beds need little covering, they often require, especially those that are bearing heavily, frequent supplies of water. It is of the greatest importance that the soil is never permitted to become dry, and water must be given as often as is needed in quantity sufficient to prevent this. The time chosen for applying water should be early in the afternoon of a sunny day, The covering on the beds will be then quite warm, and on this, not under it, the water must be sprinkled in sufficient quantity to percolate through it and gradually moisten the soil. Immediately after watering the beds they should be covered with mats to prevent the moisture evaporating, and the vapour that will be generated will result in a cool humid atmosphere under the mats and straw precisely conducive to the growth of Mushrooms, the mats to be removed in the morning. Those who are not experienced in the method of culture in question cannot understand that Mushrooms can be produced in summer on account of the heat, forgetting that by using sufficient straw, and sprinkling it, permitting at the same time free evaporation, that the beds may even be made too cold for the crop, on the same principle that ice-cold water can be produced under a tropical sun by enveloping the porous vessels in which it is stored with a medium that can be kept moist, then the constant evaporation, with the ever-attendant lowering of temperature, produces the effect desired ; still, as a rule, the crops are not profitable after the middle of June, as the Mushrooms, owing to the nitrogen they contain, speedily decay after being gathered in hot weather, and they can then no more be eaten with safety than meat can that is in a state of decomposition. If this simple fact were impressed on the minds of those Mushroom-consumers who do not always think before they eat there would be fewer records of injury resulting from partaking too freely of this esculent.

EXHAUSTED BEDS.

Mushroom beds partially exhausted by heavy and continuous bearing may be in some measure renovated by a free application of liquid manure, sufficient being given at a temperature of 100° to penetrate the entire mass of manure. The drainings from a manure heap are good for this purpose diluted until the liquid is of the colour of pale ale, 1 or 2 ozs. of common salt being added to each gallon. When the above tank liquid manure cannot be had perfectly clear soot water of the colour indicated, with salt as directed, may be advantageously applied, or an ounce of sulphate of ammonia dissolved in four gallons of water will be found equally beneficial. In the *Gardener's Chronicle*,

page 567, vol. xviii., a correspondent stated that ho
found Standen's manure valuable for the beds, and
submitted examples of Mushrooms, showing its efficacy.
These stimulants are often of great value to beds in
private gardens where a steady and prolonged supply
of Mushrooms has to be maintained; but when beds
in the open air are once fairly exhausted by heavy bearing they can seldom be profitably renovated by the use
of stimulants.

Salt has been recommended, and lest there be any
timid readers who may fear to use it at the strength
named, they may take courage from the fact that Mr.
Barter regularly uses it at the rate of a quarter of a
pound to a gallon of water, but applied, be it remembered, over the straw covering. So beneficial is salt to
Mushroom beds that it is used regularly whenever
bearing beds require watering, and it was found just
as the quantity was increased so the crops were
improved, and the Mushrooms were rendered more
white and fleshy.

GATHERING MUSHROOMS.

Different opinions are held by cultivators relative to
the best method of gathering Mushrooms. Some advo-
cate and practise cutting them, removing the stems a
few days afterwards when they can be withdrawn easily;
others pull them up, but usually do it in a very cautious
manner as if afraid of disturbing the beds and arrest-
ing the growth of further produce. When the writer
received his first lessons in Mushroom culture thirty-
five years ago it was regarded as little short of criminal
to pull Mushrooms, the orthodox plan being to cut
them. If the old practitioners who gathered the crops
so tenderly and almost in fear and trembling lest no
others should follow, could see the manner in which
Mushrooms are gathered for market they would scarcely
believe their own eyes. Not only are they torn
ruthlessly from the beds, but the roots are dug out if
they are not sufficiently broken in the process of pulling. It is usual to have two baskets, the large
Mushrooms being placed in one and the " buttons " in

the other, the soil being knocked off the roots as the work proceeds. When the stems are separated, as many are, close on the surface of the bed, leaving the stump undisturbed in the soil, this stump is at once scooped out with a knife, leaving a round open cavity in which a walnut might be placed. This to the un-initiated appears barbarous work ; it looks like spoiling the beds and preventing the production of successional crops. That it has not that effect is certain, or those to whom every pound of Mushrooms is an object would not adopt it. The result of the digging-out process is

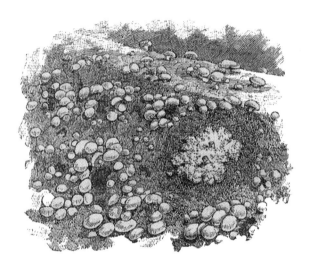

Pulling v. Cutting Mushrooms.

the direct opposite of that indicated. Instead of impair-ing the productiveness of the beds it increases it, and for a very good reason that is, however, not very easy to make intelligible to all. If the lines of communica-tion—the threads of the mycelium—from the interior to the surface of the beds which terminate in clusters of Mushrooms are not broken the strength of the beds —the Mushroom-producing force, is expended on the old stumps, and very frequently, indeed almost invari-ably, finds expression in masses of fluff of a cauliflower-like appearance, or a gigantic mass of mould or fungus. These masses if permitted speedily attain the size of dinner plates, and no more marketable Mushrooms are produced where they occur; but on the other hand, when the stumps are scooped out and the mycelium lines are severed, small tubercles form at the end of each and speedily develope into Mushrooms. The effect of this is that rings of fine produce form round each cavity, and thus the productiveness of the beds is prolonged and increased. Hundreds of gardeners know nothing of this, and there are few probably who dare practise it boldly at first; but if they were to see the thousands of indentures or cavities made in a Mushroom ridge in removing the crop, and a week hence see the fine rings of Mushrooms springing round each cavity, they would at once perceive the soundness of the practice of digging out the roots; and if for the sake of experiment some stumps were left undisturbed, and they could also see the result—the great masses of mould and no Mushrooms—they would be still further convinced that the skilled market growers have excellent reasons for the practice described.

Endeavour has been made to show as faithfully as possible in the engraving on page 57 examples of digging and non-digging the stumps out of Mushroom beds at the time of gathering the crop, and the effects in one part of Mushrooms springing round the indentures are apparent, while in the other, where the stumps were not disturbed, there is a large white mass of mould and no Mushrooms.

It may be urged against this system of gathering the crops that beds have continued bearing when a different method has been pursued. This may be the fact, as it is equally a fact that one man has travelled over the Falls of Niagara on a tight rope, and another crossed the channel in a balloon, but these are neither safe nor sure modes of transit for the majority to attempt. And in the subject in hand—obtaining the greatest quantity of Mushrooms from prepared beds—the object is to point out a path that shall be the safest and the best for all to traverse who may engage in the work.

SECURING THE CROPS—GRADES OF MUSHROOMS.

WHEN Mushrooms are gathered for market it is important, especially in cold weather, that only a small portion of a bed be uncovered at once—not more than a space over which a man can conveniently reach. From this the produce should be quickly pulled and the covering material promptly replaced. If the entire side of a long bed or ridge were uncovered before commencing gathering it would be exposed so long as to cause such a loss of heat as would seriously check the succeeding crop and impair the value of the bed ; while even if the weather were not cold, yet dry, there would be a loss of moisture that it is most desirable to conserve. Mushroom beds in bearing must always be moist, many being kept too dry ; and it is decidedly faulty practice to expedite the escape of moisture from them, and then have to make good the loss with the aid of the watering pot, as this, to say the least, involves needless labour, while the beds are not in such a satisfactory state as they would have been had they not been permitted to become dry.

It is not unusual for 9 or 10 lbs. of Mushrooms to be secured at one gathering from the small space above indicated ; and as these represent as many shillings, the work, if sometimes of a cooling nature, as it is during a period of frost and snow, is yet not disagreeable to the workman who is gathering his own crops. During mild weather in autumn and late spring it is customary, in the case of young beds, to clear off the crops twice a week. During colder weather or with older beds the produce is only collected once a week. As a rule a productive bed will yield ten gatherings, seven of them full, the first and two last lighter by comparison.

In securing the crops it is convenient, as has been previously suggested, for the workman to have two baskets, one for the cups and buttons, the other for the broilers. This separation, when the Mushrooms are first handled, results in a saving of time at the weighing table, a matter of some moment when several bushels have to be divided into pounds, arranged in punnets, and tied down separately in the shortest possible time. This is the form in which all Mushrooms are sent to market. They are packed with their stems entire just as gathered from the beds minus the soil that is drawn out with the roots, and which is shaken off as the pulling proceeds. They are snatched rapidly, and, as an inexperienced on-looker would think, roughly, from the ridges ; the collector always having a knife in his hand with which, for the reason previously stated, he quickly scoops out the stumps of any of the clusters that snap off close to the surface.

RETAINING THE STEMS OF MUSHROOMS.

The retention of the whole of the stems obviously benefits the grower, as they materially increase the weight of the crop, and the practice is also advantageous to greengrocers and others who make large purchases in the market with the object of retailing the Mushrooms to their customers. Consumers are in one sense, and that not an unimportant one, benefited, too, by the custom in question. No doubt there are readers who will be glad to know in what manner the two last-named classes can derive any advantages by purchasing what cannot be eaten, as before the Mushrooms are cooked the stalks must be cut off and thrown away— unless, indeed, they are utilised for making ketchup, which is only practicable when they are collected in large quantities. The benefit arising from retaining the stems is this : Mushrooms keep sound and wholesome much longer than if the stalks were cut off. This is a distinct advantage to the retail vendor, as his goods are thereby rendered less perishable, and his liability to loss by a slow sale is materially reduced. If the vendor derives benefit by the freshness and good quality

of his wares so also must the consumer, and by purchasing Mushrooms in their entirety he has them as
far as is possible in possession of their full flavour;
whereas if divested of their stalks a few days previous
to use they are insipid if not worse, as their virtues have
escaped through their wounds, incipient decay has been
accelerated, their constituents have been changed, and
their wholesomeness impaired. Fresh Mushrooms—
true samples of the Fungus, Agaricus campestris—are
quite safe; it is only false Mushrooms that are question-
able or dangerous.

DIFFERENT GRADES OF MUSHROOMS.

There are three distinct grades of Mushrooms in
demand in the markets. These are known as Buttons,

Cups, and Broilers, and each
is in request for different culinary purposes. "Buttons"
are Mushrooms in embryo—
that is to say, the cap of the
pileus is united to the stalk,
and the laminæ or gills are
not visible. It does not matter what the size of these
young Mushrooms may be,
whether of the dimensions of
a small Cobnut or a large

Fig. 1.—Buttons.

Walnut, if the gills are veiled they are still buttons.
"Cups" are a step advanced in development. Immediately the membranous covering that unites the hood
with the stem breaks, the term "buttons" is no longer
applicable, and the young Mushrooms are recognised
as "cups," but only retain that designation so long as
they are unopened and do not show more than a ring
of the laminæ half an inch in diameter. When they
expand fully and assume the form of an inverted tea-
saucer, showing the gills clearly, they are matured for
culinary purposes and become broilers; but they are not
perfect for the purpose of reproduction, as spores are
not distributed until the laminæ have changed from a
lively pink colour to a brownish black, and they

should be gathered, sold, and eaten before that change occurs.

RELATIVE VALUE OF MUSHROOMS.

As there are different grades of Mushrooms so also these grades have different values. As a rule, when large Mushrooms or broilers realise 1s. per lb. the cups will sell for 1s. 3d. and the buttons for 1s. 6d. It does not follow, however, that the latter are the more profitable to the cultivator. Probably the reverse is the case, as the enormously greater weight of the broilers more than compensates for the reduction in their value as determined by their price per pound; but even here there is a set-off, as if no buttons were gathered, but all were allowed to expand, the beds would be more quickly exhausted, and instead of yielding nine or ten crops they would probably only produce six or seven. The practice, then, of gathering all the grades is a safe

Fig. 2.—Cups.

one, and, as has been shown in preceding pages, is sufficiently profitable, while the market demand is met in a manner that is satisfactory all round. It is well, therefore, when securing the produce to clear all off that is readily marketable either as buttons, cups, or broilers.

The different grades of Mushrooms are represented in the annexed engravings, which also show the manner in

which the produce is arranged in punnets.   Fig. 1 indicates buttons; fig. 2 cups, and fig. 3 broilers.   Details

Fig. 3.—Broilers.

of the methods of packing and preparing for sale will
be given in the next chapter.

MARKETING THE CROPS—PUNNETS.

As previously observed Mushrooms are packed in punnets, and a few particulars relative to these articles that are sold by millions annually at such a cheap rate will not be uninteresting, but, on the contrary, may be serviceable to many readers of this treatise. Vast numbers of gardeners even know little or nothing about the manufacture of the small, handy, and cheap chip punnets that are seen in nearly every green-grocer's shop and fruiterer's window ; and if they were asked where they could be obtained, and at what price, it is certain that not one in twenty would be able to give an accurate reply. This being so, and the statement cannot be controverted, the need of information on the matter becomes apparent. Among other places where these useful articles—indeed, indispensable to the Mushroom grower—are made, Brentford and Hammersmith must be named as "seats of manufacture," and it appears as natural for the industrial population, the old and young of both sexes, to make them there as it is for fowls to scratch in seed beds or boys to take Apples when they are offered, or when "nobody is looking." It is only by much practice and dexterity that the thick shavings can be so deftly worked into baskets as, when sold at the current rates, to leave a margin of profit behind them. Many, however, are made in the evening after the regular labour of the day has ended, and thus odd moments are commendably turned to account, while children are taught habits of industry and are content to earn a few pence at the work in question. Thus it is that the punnets cost so little as often to be given away with fruit that is sold in them. But they are not quite given away with Mushrooms, as it is the practice in weighing them into pounds to throw a punnet into the scale and not on the side containing the weights ; still, if the scales were balanced with the greatest exactitude, the purchaser would not give more than a farthing for a punnet, and it is worth that for the convenience of carrying the Mushrooms home, apart from any use to which it may be applied afterwards. But in practice the weighing cannot be done with such great nicety, and as the "draw" of the scale is always in favour of

Punnets.

the purchaser he practically gets his little basket for nothing. They are sold in rolls of three dozens, as represented in the annexed sketch, which also affords an idea of the number required and used in a Mushroom-growing establishment. They are employed in three different sizes—namely, for "buttons," 5 inches in diameter and $3\frac{1}{2}$ inches deep, and known as "deep

F

pounds," for "cups," 6½ inches in diameter and 2 inches deep, known as "flat pounds;" and for broilers, 5½ inches across and an inch deep, sold as "halves." The price of course varies with the size, deep pounds and flat pounds being usually obtainable for 6s., and halves 4s. per gross. With the object of rendering these notes substantially useful it may be stated that the stock from which the figure was prepared was obtained at the prices quoted from Mr. P. Nicholls, 377, Goldhawk Road, Hammersmith. It may be that other makers may sell them even cheaper, and if so they need have no difficulty in making the facts known ; in the meantime Mr. Nicholls will presumably not seriously object to the mention of his name in connection with this apparently simple yet certainly not unimportant subject, for the question of punnets is one of the essentials in the industry of Mushroom-growing for market purposes.

PACKING MUSHROOMS.

When large quantities are gathered it is customary for two men to be engaged in weighing and packing— one sorts them from the hampers, quickly divests them of any loose particles of soil or manure from the tops or roots, and weighs them into pounds; the other places them in the punnets and ties them down. Packing must be neatly done, as a little care in this respect adds materially to the saleable value of the stock, while scarcely any more time is incurred in the process than by doing the work roughly and without thought. It is not the habit of experienced growers of garden produce for the London market to place the best samples at the bottom. If the produce is good all through, as it ought to be and often is, still care is exercised to select either fruit or Mushrooms of uniform size for the uppermost layer. It is from this practice that the very expressive word "topper" originated as denoting anything of exceptional merit; and though the term is perhaps not found in all dictionaries it is much more than a provincialism, as it is widely used and well understood over the greater part of the country. In packing Mushrooms, then, do not forget the "toppers," but let the work when done appear as represented in the figures on pages 61, 62, and 63.   Provided the whole produce is saleable, as it ought to be, and must be if a vendor is to maintain a position, there is no more deception in arranging the specimens neatly and attractively than there is in dressing a horse for the fair, or legs of mutton or poultry for the market.   But all must be done fairly and honestly.   The man who fails in this respect by hiding unsaleable produce will sooner or later be inevitably shunned—unable to dispose of whatever he has

Packing Mushrooms for market.

to sell, and serve him right.   The best of garden produce may be seriously deteriorated, because made more or less unsightly by rough usage and defective packing. In fact, it may be stated without hesitation that hundreds of pounds are lost annually by want of care in this respect, and vendors are disappointed while purchasers are dissatisfied.   It becomes necessary, therefore, to emphasise the importance of placing whatever

is good in the market in the best manner, including
Mushrooms, as by this course purchasers are attracted,
whereas by the opposite habit of careless preparation
and arrangement they are certainly repelled.

PACKING THE PUNNETS.

After the Mushrooms are papered neatly and secured
with raffia, which is the best and cheapest tying material, the punnets are packed in light yet sufficiently
strong boxes, such as anyone can make who can use
a saw, hammer, and nails, appearance here being of
little moment. Neither is it material that the boxes
be of a particular size ; still, it may be submitted that
those of the following dimensions are found convenient
for moving and arranging in vans without loss of space
—3 feet 2 inches long, 1 foot 11 inches wide, and 1 foot
4 inches deep, an inch batten being nailed across the
inside of each end 8 inches from the bottom. This is
for supporting a floor or shelf after the bottom of the
box has been occupied with punnets. From fifty-six
to sixty punnets can be accommodated in what may
be termed the two layers in a box of this kind ; and a
little clean hay being used if needed for making the
punnets firm, with a few strips of deal tacked across
the top for protection, the produce may be sent any
reasonable distance without fear of injury. Salesmen
in London are glad to dispose of good Mushrooms, and
the leading greengrocers in the large provincial cities
and towns can rarely obtain sufficient to meet the demand
for them that already exists, and which is sure to increase
in the future.

TWELVE MODES OF GROWING MUSHROOMS.

ALTHOUGH undoubtedly the method previously described of growing Mushrooms in the open air is the best for producing them in large quantities for commercial purposes, yet with the object of as far as possible meeting the requirements of persons, variously situated and circumstanced, who may desire to grow a few Mushrooms, several other methods shall be advanced for providing them, in the hope that some one or other will be adaptable to the means and conveniences of every one who may read these pages. No fanciful modes will be advanced, nor systems promulgated that have not been subjected to the test of experience, but, on the contrary, except where otherwise stated, every plan submitted has been proved by the writer to answer the purpose required when fairly carried out. The first six methods were first brought into notice by one of the best practical gardeners of the century, the late Mr. Robert Fish, and made known to the world twenty years ago. As they are much too good and suggestive to be lost, they are essentially reproduced here.

1. Finding in the month of August a good quantity of short flaky manure from the stable, I had this wheeled to an open spot, shaken and broken well with the fork, and then built firmly in a ridge a yard wide at bottom and a yard high to the apex. Contrary to my expectation this dryish wasted material heated rather violently. An old practitioner advised boring it full of holes to let the heat out; but, as I considered that the material was rather of an open nature, and boring holes would make it opener still, and thus at first rather increase the heat, I preferred beating the bed hard all over, and sprinkling a little soil over it to

keep the air out instead of letting it in ; in a short
time the bed gradually decreased in temperature ; and
when it was about 90°, or the heat of new milk, I
inserted pieces of good spawn every 9 inches equally
all over it and about half an inch below the surface,
beating that surface well again. In a few days
the bed was fit for earthing up, the thermometer
just beneath the surface registering 88°. The garden
soil being well stored with manurial matter, and as a
necessary consequence not deficient in worms and
slugs—the former of which would have prevented the
soil of the bed being firm enough, and the latter have
feasted on the Mushrooms—I dug down between 2 and
3 feet, and got some stiffish fresh soil from the bottom
of the trench, with which I cased the bed about
2½ inches thick, kneading it in as compactly as possible,
watering it, and making it smooth and hard with a
clean spade, and then threw over it a little loose litter
to prevent the sun and air cracking it. As the nights
got colder a little more litter was used, and ultimately
drawn straw to throw off the wet. During autumn,
winter, and spring the inside of the bed varied from
85° down to 60°, and the surface ranged from 65° to
48°. In seven weeks from the insertion of the spawn
Mushrooms made their appearance, and the bed continued productive for the best part of a twelvemonth.

2. At the same time I put up another bed made of
dung that had been worked sweet for a hotbed, but was
rather moist, mixed with more exhausted rather wet
material from the linings above referred to. This
heated rather violently at first, but when it declined it
felt very clammy and wet ; in fact, when squeezed
firmly, a drop of liquid would soon trickle through the
fingers. I considered that pieces of spawn would soon
perish when put into such material. Every piece was
therefore firmly wrapped in a ball of dryish material
similar to that which I had made the first bed of, each
of these balls being larger than my two fists. A hole
was made for them, and they were firmly inserted in
the bed, and covered by an inch or two of the moist
dung. This bed yielded Mushrooms so large and so
thick that the difficulty was in cooking them. The

spawn ran freely in the loose dry litter, and when it got to the richer, moister material of the bed it gave succulence and size to the Mushrooms.

3. Having a lot of tree leaves in November heating nicely and sweetly, I made a bed of them in a shed about 18 inches deep. On this I put 6 inches of horse droppings, and when the heat was all right spawned and treated in the usual way. This bed retained its heat for a very long period, but the Mushrooms, though good, were inclined to spread and be rather thin. On a similar bed, after spawning, I put an inch of rich moist cow dung, plastering it all over, and when a little dry soiling up in the usual way. Here the Mushrooms were round and thick, and ever since, when I want fleshy thick Mushrooms in shallow beds in Mushroom houses, I use the cow dung as a surfacing.

4. Though approving, for shallow beds in houses, of the drying and turning of horse droppings, yet I was so convinced that this might be done to an injurious extent so as to deprive the manure of much of its nutritive qualities, that I tried a bed without giving the droppings any preparation at all. These droppings were brought direct from the stable, rejecting those that were extra wet, and having as much bulk of litter as droppings. These were spread into a bed about 3 inches thick in an open shed, well trodden and beaten, and thinly covered with fibry soil, which was dry rather than moist. In three or four days 2 inches more of the droppings, &c., were added, and another sprinkling of soil and beating given, and so the process went on until in about three weeks I had a bed nearly 15 inches deep. Using the manure rather dry, with the addition of the dry earth, and the thorough beating each time, prevented the bed heating very violently, though it was so hot as to require to stand the best part of a fortnight before it could be trusted with the spawn. This bed was earthed up in the usual manner with fresh soil from the bottom of a deep trench in the kitchen garden, and yielded continuously for a long period fine crops of Mushrooms. A piece at one end was surfaced with 2 inches of cow dung that had lain

in a heap three or four months and had lost its rankness; from this part the Mushrooms were thick and round, and the cook complained that it was impossible to cook them thoroughly. With suitable protection of litter and mats these beds produced liberally all the winter.

5. Fearing that these beds referred to might be injured by some sudden extreme frost, and knowing that uncovering such beds out of doors was no very pleasant affair on a rainy or a snowy day in winter, I also made beds on raised platforms in stokeholes, so that the fire used for keeping out frost in the houses in winter would keep the beds all right. I found that these beds were the better for a moist surfacing after spawning, and that they did very well with a little covering of litter to keep an equal temperature until the stokehole became too hot, when forcing the houses commenced. I also made beds on the floors of vineries and below the stages of greenhouses, and found they gave much less trouble than in any other circumstances, as little covering was necessary, and could all be done in the dry and comfortably. Of course, when the heat of the vinery was raised to 70° or so there was an end of fine fleshy Mushrooms.

6. Among other methods I tried them in portable wooden boxes 3 feet in length, 15 inches wide, and the same in depth; and also in large pots, using chiefly horse droppings and dried cow dung, and found them useful when placed in a forcing house not too hot, or at the warmest end in a greenhouse. An amateur who would be beaten by nothing had an almost constant supply from large pots all the year round, and had neither a close shed nor glass house to keep them in, and the droppings of only one pony to depend upon; but he had a good deep cellar, cool in summer and warm in winter, and there his pots were placed when prepared and finished. From him I learnt the importance of such a cellar, or a cool airy place beneath the thick shade of trees, for growing Mushrooms in summer.

7. The following method of growing Mushrooms with the aid of sawdust was described in 1881 by Mr. John

Woollam ; it has not been tested by the writer, but those who have the means for carrying it out may possibly be induced to give it a trial. Cocoa-nut fibre refuse would doubtless answer at the least equally well used in the same manner. " I wish to state a valuable use we make of sawdust here. It has for several years been very much employed as bedding for horses. Two years ago I found in the manure from such bedding after lying in a heap a short time what appeared good Mushroom spawn ; and as we had difficulty in procuring sufficient droppings for making Mushroom beds I determined to try a bed of sawdust manure, and fully made up my mind for a good crop of bad fungus ; but, to my agreeable surprise, it turned out the best bed of Mushrooms that we have had for years. Since then I have used nothing else when I wish to make up a bed. I have the manure fresh, make the lower part of the bed, then screen part of the sawdust out of the remainder of the manure, and add about 2 inches of the screened droppings on the top of the bed, make it thoroughly firm, then insert the spawn, soil it over, smooth the surface with the back of a spade, and in a month or five weeks I have a fine crop of strong brown-capped Mushrooms. I had insufficient spawn last spring, and after making a bed neglected to spawn it, as we had such a large crop on hand. In a few weeks the Mushrooms began appearing ; I then soiled it over, and had as large a crop from that bed as any of the others, but of a smaller size. Possibly this information may be of service to some readers."

8. Another novel method of growing Mushrooms is practised successfully in Sheffield. It is described as follows by Mr. Woodcock, himself a skilful cultivator and undoubtedly an accurate writer :—" There are now (December, 1882), in full bearing at ' Broomfield,' Sheffield (the residence of B. P. Broomhead, Esq.), several Mushroom beds which for quantity and quality of the produce I have not before seen equalled, except in the case of Mr. J. Barter's outdoor beds. Mr. Walker, the able gardener at Broomfield, tells me that the material of which these beds are composed consists solely of sphagnum moss imported from Germany,

where it has been artificially dried and afterwards compressed by hydraulic power into cakes or bales of about 1 cwt. each, and which are sold as a patented bedding material for horses, &c. Mr. Broomhead purchased a quantity for use in his stables, where its merits are appreciated, as it speedily and readily absorbs all the drainage and ammonia, and keeps the stable free from all unpleasant smells. Thinking it would be a good material for Mushroom-growing, Mr. Walker made up some beds with it, which have succeeded beyond his expectations. He says he has never before had beds which have been so quick in coming into bearing or so lastingly productive. He commenced gathering Mushrooms in five weeks from the making-up of the beds, and when I saw them he had been gathering from them every day for five weeks, and the beds then were quite covered with fine Mushrooms, which were very thick and solid. He also showed me a box which by way of experiment he had filled with moss which had not been used in the stables, but which he had saturated with stable drainage from a tank where it is collected. This upon being made up into the box heated very strongly, so that he had to wait a number of days for the heat to subside before spawning; but when I first saw it the spawn had run through it, and Mushrooms were appearing apparently as thickly and as freely as upon the other beds. On a subsequent examination there was no doubt that the experiment was a great success, as the box was crowded with splendid Mushrooms."

9. The simple plan now to be noticed has been practised for years with the most satisfactory results. Any time after midsummer, when Melons and Cucumbers grown in frames on beds of stable manure and leaves are showing signs of exhaustion, and when it is no longer profitable to give copious waterings daily, insert large lumps of spawn 3 or 4 inches deep all over the beds, pressing a handful of horse droppings with the soil firmly round them. If the bed is kept moist, but not decidedly wet, the mycelium will spread rapidly, the temperature at that period of the year (August) being suitable, and in due time a fine crop of Mushrooms

will be produced. The foliage of the Cucumbers
and Melons prevents the sun parching the surface of
the beds for a time, and after the plants are removed
the beds should be covered with hay. If good spawn
is used, and proper attention given to condition of the
beds as to moisture, it is not improbable that the
Mushroom crop, which has cost so little to produce,
will be as much valued as the Cucumbers and Melons
were. Frames full of Mushrooms have been had for
months, even through the winter, by this the easiest of all
systems of culture. For the encouragement of those
who may hesitate to adopt a plan so simple as this is, it
may be stated that Dr. Hogg, of the *Journal of Horticulture,* did not disdain to gather his whole supply of
Mushrooms from a common frame of the kind indicated
during a period of six months in 1881-82.

10. Many persons who have dung beds desire to
occupy the frames after the Melons are over with other
plants and crops than Mushrooms. The space may be
needed for propagating and protecting flowering plants
in the autumn, or for accommodating young Cauli-
flower plants, or salads. Even such persons may have
acceptable dishes of Mushrooms from the beds, but
outside the frames instead of inside. All they have to
do is to press large pieces of spawn in the sides of the
beds a foot from the ground in July, and a week or two
afterwards, when the mycelium is spreading, form
sloping banks of soil round the beds. In due time
Mushrooms will be plentiful, huge clusters often forming, and with protection continue being produced for
several weeks. Many dishes of the finest of Mushrooms
have been gathered by this easy method of culture—so
easy that it is liable to be overlooked by many; hence
its record here.

11. Mushrooms are grown in houses of various kinds
—some well and others ill adapted for the purpose.
Sudden fluctuations of temperature and changes of
atmosphere are inimical to Mushrooms. Some stables
are eminently suited for producing crops, as also are
cellars. Brick buildings exposed to the sun with thin
walls and slated or tiled roofs are the worst of structures for the work in question. With the best of skill

and materials good crops cannot be produced in such
places.   One example will suffice to confirm this statement.   At Longleat such a house was erected for
Mushrooms, but none was forthcoming, and never
would have been under the circumstances.   An able
gardener, Mr. Taylor, on entering on his charge, was
quick to perceive the defect and to apply the remedy.
He thatched the walls thickly, and filled the roof with
straw, thus securing an equable temperature, and then
had no more difficulty in growing Mushrooms in the
house than growing Onions in the garden.   In Mushroom houses the beds are made in bins on the floor
and on shelves above it, the beds being not less than a
foot thick.   When the floors of the elevated bins are
formed of strong battens double beds may be had.
" Never heard of such," some reader may ejaculate.
Possibly not, but if he will adopt the plan of Mr. Gray
of Sudbrooke Holme, near Lincoln, he may see them.
On this gardener spawning some beds in the usual way
on the surface, it occurred to him to press some pieces
of spawn between the battens in the underneath side
of the beds as well.   The experiment proved a great
success, the crops from the under side of the bed being
in every respect equal to those produced on the surface,
thus forming, without any increase of material, what
may be accurately described as DOUBLE MUSHROOM BEDS.
Now that Mr. Gray's experience is recorded other cultivators will doubtless endeavour in a similar manner
to increase the supply of Mushrooms from elevated
beds.

12. An exceedingly simple method of raising Mushrooms remains to be noticed.   It was first described by
a famous gardener, the late Mr. Errington, and the
merits of the plan have been well proved.   " I desire
to point to a plan by which Mushrooms may be had
with ease and certainty from the beginning of July
until the end of October, and that with little trouble,
cost, or skill.   I have a wall facing the west, covered
from one end to the other with trained choice Pears.
This wall, about 150 feet long, has a coping projecting
about 8 inches, and, of course, what with the Pear
leaves and the coping, the drip is thrown nearly a foot

from the wall at its base. At the foot of this wall in May a labourer dug out one single spit of soil in a continuous line and close to its base, and having some droppings in a shed, half dry, intended for Mushroom culture, he filled this trench with them, raising the surface above the ground level, and sloping it away from the wall. It was now well trodden, and the excavated soil cased over it 2 inches in thickness. Lumps of spawn were immediately planted with a dibble at half a yard apart, and the work was thus completed. We never took any further notice of it until July, when the Mushrooms began pushing through in all directions. The surface was covered with weeds left purposely, and the shade of which they seemed to enjoy; as, however, they became robbers I thought it expedient to remove them, and the surface is and has been exposed. They are as fine as it is possible for Mushrooms to be, but I daresay would be none the worse for a thin covering of straw or litter. I was not at all astonished at the success of the simple affair, although several knowing persons in the gardening way have appeared so. This shows how imperfectly still Mushroom culture is understood. The fact is this : their culture depends on such simple principles that their requirements have ever been overrated, and they may even be grown in the manner indicated by the side of a row of Peas, Brussels Sprouts, or any crop that will at once afford shade from the sun in summer and shelter from drenching rains."

MUSHROOMS IN PASTURES.

MANY persons are desirous of establishing Mushrooms in pastures, and the following method submitted by Mr. Barter as the simplest and best for accomplishing the object will not be unacceptable to those who are interested in this aspect of culture.

Manure should be prepared as if to be made into a bed (see page 28), and when it is in the right condition remove squares of turf the size of a spade and about 3 inches deep, taking out at the same time sufficient soil to admit of a large forkful of manure. In the centre of this place a quarter of a brick of good spawn, and tread the whole in firmly, replacing the turf at once, and beating it down so that it is as hard and level as before removal. Any time from the middle of May to the middle of June will be suitable for doing this, as at that time the temperature of the earth is usually sufficient to incite the growth of the mycelium, while at the same time the requisite degree of moisture is generally provided. A very good index of this, however, will be afforded by the state of the turf. Should the grass show any signs of dying it must be watered carefully, giving just sufficient for keeping the grass green.

The most suitable pastures for Mushrooms are those where the turf is old and the earth a mass of fibrous roots, the soil of medium texture, and the subsoil porous. In pastures of this kind one spawning would probably suffice, as the mycelium would become established in the roots of the grass, except, perhaps, during an unusually wet season. In view of this contingency it is well to choose slight elevations rather than hollows or depressions in the pasture, and it is advisable also to have the prepared places as close together as possible, even if spawn is not inserted in all of them at the same time. Mushrooms grow freely in light soil, but if plentiful are usually small.

In heavy soils where the subsoil is not porous it would probably be necessary to insert spawn every year. The Mushrooms, however, would generally be much heavier than in light land, and perhaps more than repay the difference in the cost incurred by the yearly spawning. Meadows which are naturally wet, and districts where the rainfall is great, cannot be expected to give a satisfactory return for the outlay incurred in labour and material for accomplishing the work in question. It is impossible to explain precisely and in an intelligible manner the pastures that are adapted for Mushrooms or the reverse, but the point can be determined by a few well-conducted experiments on the lines above indicated.

THE INFLUENCE OF SALT ON MUSHROOMS.

While it is well known that a large quantity of salt applied to gathered Mushrooms accelerates their decay, as in the manufacture of ketchup, yet evidence is not wanting showing that salt has a compensating influence in facilitating their growth. Attention was directed to this matter upwards of thirty years ago by Mr. Brownell, a solicitor near Chester, who has recorded that Mr. Joshua Starkey, a respectable farmer living in Agden, sowed on his grass and pasture lands in February a ton weight of common salt. To his surprise a large crop of excellent Mushrooms made their appearance in the autumn. What makes the above more remarkable is that he sowed one old pasture completely over with the salt, as well as several portions of other fields, which had recently been laid down for grass. The old pasture produced an enormous crop of Mushrooms, and the parts of fields which he sowed produced more or less; whilst upon the other parts of the same fields, upon which no salt had been sown, not a Mushroom was to be found. A farmer of the name of Stannier, residing in the same neighbourhood, also mixed a quantity of salt with some compost (ditch scourings, &c.), and laid it during the winter months on one of his fields.

He gathered a large crop of Mushrooms where the compost had been spread—indeed he states that he actually mowed them with a scythe off the land, and that he sold in one week twelve hampers of them at £1 each. It seems to be a fact, well known at the salt works at Northwich, that salt is an article capable of producing Mushrooms when applied to grass lands; for when Mr. Starkey's servant fetched from that place the salt which he used he was told he might expect a crop of Mushrooms.

Mr. Henry Galton wrote as follows in January, 1881, on the influence of salt in promoting the growth of Mushrooms in pastures :—" One field here has this year produced such great numbers of Mushrooms, and so many people came to gather them early in the morning, that the farmer had to stop the practice, as the Oats were greatly injured. This abundance was attributed to salt having been strewn over the land with the corn, which seems all that is required here to induce the growth of Mushrooms. I have seen salt strewn on meadow land with the same result, especially where cattle graze. About Lent seems the best time to strew it over pastures. The manure of cattle greatly increases the number of the Mushrooms, but I cannot understand their appearing in a field where only a slight dressing of manure was placed as usually used by farmers for killing wireworms. I have seen the same result when Sainfoin that had been down nine or ten years was broken up, salt being employed for fear of wireworm. I would advise gardeners to try the experiment in parks where cattle are kept."

On this subject Mr. Gilbert, of Welton, near Lincoln, wrote in January, 1883 :—" My observation tends to confirm what is very generally firmly believed here— namely, the importance of salt in the production of Mushrooms. Some nine or ten years since a field in the occupation of the late W. Marshall, Esq., of this place produced (to my own knowledge) many bushels of Mushrooms both before and after the Wheat was carted. The cause was attributed to the use of salt. Subsequently Mr. Drayton, also of this place, gathered an incredible quantity from a stubble field which had been salted in the spring. I had some years since an Asparagus bed made with stable, pig, and other manure. It was occasionally salted, and one morning in April I found there a Mushroom as large as a dinner plate, with many others from 2 to 4 or 5 inches across, and many gatherings were had from this bed during the summer. With the object of gaining further evidence, a little before six o'clock one morning I went to a place where I knew I should meet with some agricultural labourers on their way to work. I found three. No. 1 could relate all the particulars that I have stated about Mr. Marshall's field, and also described what I know to be true, that Mr. Kemp, who is Mr. Marshall's successor in the farm, had a very considerable quantity of Mushrooms in the autumn of 1882 from two or three Wheat fields which had been sown with salt. His colleague No. 2 described how another farmer also had a quantity from Wheat stubbles two or three years since after the land had been salted. No. 3, a very respectable man, described how Mr. J. Coney obtained a large crop of Mushrooms from among Mangold Wurzels in a field which had been heavily salted. He also said that many years ago, after some alterations of the churchyard, the late Robert Medley, Esq., carted some soil and mixed with other soil and salt, and after remaining some time, perhaps a year, spread it on the land, and a profusion of Mushrooms was the result. I have since spoken to Mr. Drayton, son of the gentleman before mentioned, and he also had last year (1882) a quantity of Mushrooms from corn land that had been salted. Last year in Mr. Kemp's field there were places that seemed to have been soddened with a free application of salt, and Mushrooms grew profusely in rings round those places. The land I have mentioned is rather light and of a loamy character, and did not produce Mushrooms before salt was applied. These are striking facts, and it is singular that salt should have such influence."

The above evidence relative to the usefulness of salt as a manure for Mushrooms is not unworthy of notice, and more of a similar character could be adduced. I am satisfied that, on dry soils at any rate, salting the land is favourable for this crop, I am well acquainted with a small farm in a large agricultural district on which Mushrooms grow freely both in the pasture and arable land. I have seen many bushels gathered from amongst Potatoes and Turnips, in some places Mushrooms springing up as thick as they could stand for yards together. It is on this farm only that Mushrooms grow. The soil of the surrounding fields is of precisely the same nature—medium hazel loam well drained; in fact, first-rate Potatoe and Barley land, growing also good crops of Wheat. The only difference in the management of the land is that on the farm where the Mushrooms grow the farmer has been in the habit of sowing 2 cwt. of salt per acre for a number of years, so that the land is thus impregnated with salt. I once inserted some lumps of spawn in a pasture on this farm, and the same day another portion in an adjoining field that had not been salted. The weather being favourable Mushrooms followed in both instances, but they were both much finer and more numerous in the field that had been regularly salted than in the other. The district is, however, a dry one, and similar results might not follow in a wet locality. Nor must it be supposed that salt of itself can produce Mushrooms; the spores or mycelium must first be in the soil before the crops can grow, but that this manure accelerates their growth appears as certain as that phosphatic manures facilitate the growth of Clover in pastures.

WHO MAY GROW MUSHROOMS.

FARMERS.—Since from various causes the earth's products have been so restricted in value, many remedies more or less practical have been suggested. Farmers have been advised to turn their fields into gardens. Able speeches have been delivered on this matter, and equally able articles have appeared in the press, while books have been published on this subject, some of which have imparted sound and useful information; but in none of them has the question of Mushroom culture been fully and practically treated from a commercial point of view. Yet there are no members of the community which have the same means for growing Mushrooms profitably as those farmers have who employ several horses and reside within easy distance of a railway. Let no gardener who has failed to grow Mushrooms regard this as a mere fanciful theory or wild dream. On the contrary, it is perfectly practicable, and there are numbers of men who possess the means and intelligence for growing Mushrooms in abundance if they will follow instructions perseveringly. Failures they may incur at the first, or they may not; but if they do incur them the means that produced them have only to be ascertained and avoided in the next attempt, and they will certainly then be within " measurable distance" of success. It should always be remembered—and let this be impressed on the rising generation especially with all the emphasis that language and example can afford—that by no class of men have failures been so numerous, so great, even almost crushing, as by those who have eventually won the most brilliant successes. Innumerable instances of this might be quoted, for in every calling, vocation, and profession history teems with examples of those who have fought their way in peace and in war,

through obstacles that to the timid, halting, and hesi-
tating appeared invulnerable, and in the end the goal
was reached, and perseverance in turning failures to
account had its reward. This is true of great things
and in small, from making railways to growing Mushrooms ; and if in the latter work "a carpenter" can
succeed, as has been shown he has succeeded, why
should farmers and others more or less intimate with
the cultivation of the land fail? Farmers, then, can
grow Mushrooms if they will, and they have little to
lose in making the attempt. At present the manure
from their yards and stables is carted into heaps, and
after it has partially decayed is turned over. Now, by
preparing it for Mushroom beds it would only need
turning when fresh for the purpose of sweetening it,
instead of deferring the work until shortly before the
manure is applied to the land, for it must be remembered that when the Mushroom beds have ceased bearing the manure is in proper condition, without further
turnings, for incorporating with the soil.

Market Gardeners who reside near towns and can
obtain a plentiful supply of suitable manure will find a
well-managed system of Mushroom culture greatly to
their advantage. No argument is necessary to prove
the truth of this statement, for it is supported by the
incontrovertible evidence of facts. For years past
some of the leading market gardeners in what may be
termed the metropolitan district have systematically
purchased large quantities of manure fresh from the
London stables with the object of first producing from
t valuable crops of Mushrooms, and then when it has
decayed utilising it for the land. By no other means
could they have secured such a substantial return for
the outlay invested in manure. For general cropping
purposes it is essential that manure be more or less
decomposed before being mixed with the soil. Why,
then, should it not be utilised during the process of
decomposition instead of the heaps lying barren for
three or four months ? If there were no crop that it
would sustain during fermentation, then there would
be no choice ; but it is well known that by its agency
valuable crops of Cucumbers, Melons, Tomatoes, &c.,

are produced in frames, and it ought to be equally
widely known that it will afford still more valuable
crops of Mushrooms in the open air. Then when the
crops have been gathered the manure that has produced
them is ready for use for producing other crops, and
few cultivators of gardens object to a supply of dung
from hotbeds. If a system of culture is profitable near
London, where land is more highly rented than any-
where else in the kingdom, why should not a similar
practice be at least equally lucrative in the environs of
other cities and towns where land is less dear and
manure often equally cheap? It cannot be said that
the climate of London is specially favourable for the
growth of Mushrooms, for the whole system is artificial.
The climate for this crop is made, not naturally existent,
and with manure rightly prepared and used, the same
degree of heat can be produced in the beds, and the
same conditions of temperature and moisture surrounding them by coverings of straw can be as well provided
two hundred miles from London as at Chiswick,
Fulham, Camberwell, or Paddington.

Florists and Small Nurserymen might also benefit
themselves considerably by making Mushroom culture
a part of their business. Manure they must have for
applying to the soil, or it would soon become exhausted
by the constant removal of flowers, trees, and shrubs.
As, then, the maintenance of the soil's fertility is
imperative if the land is to be remuneratively occupied,
manure becomes a necessity. Let it be purchased
in the state above indicated, and prepared in the
manner described, and the crops of Mushrooms that it
is capable of producing will more than defray all the
cost of purchase and labour, and the residue (the old
beds) will afford a dressing for the land which cannot
easily be excelled for trees and flowers. There is so
much to be gained in Mushroom culture by those who
succeed in the work, and so little to be lost by those
who essay their cultivation on a limited scale at first,
that the experiment is well worthy of being tried by
that large number of individuals whose livelihood depends on rendering the small plots of ground at their
disposal to the fullest extent productive. In those

districts where there is a great demand for such hardy
popular flowers as Pansies, Pinks, Sweet Williams,
Phloxes, &c., the decayed manure from Mushroom
beds will be found of great value. Near London such
manure is in constant demand, and is largely used for
those crops, tons of it being also used for growing
Mustard and Cress for the metropolitan and provincial
markets.

For this purpose alone it is worthy of note that one
grower derived £1500 last year from an acre of Mushrooms, and with the material from the spent beds
grows Mustard, or rather Rape and Cress, on a scale
that enables him to send at the least five hundred
dozens of punnets weekly to Covent Garden, for which
he receives as many shillings in return, and altogether
a thousand dozens of punnets are sent to London
daily during the early spring months. This is a most
profitable crop, and nothing produces it so quicky and
well as the rather dry sifted manure from old Mushroom
beds.*

Why cannot growers of these and other crops every-
where provide a supply of this manure that suits them
so well, since a substantial profit is capable of being
realised in the work of its preparation ? It is certain
that if by attention and perseverance good Mushroom
beds are produced the returns will be great, and not
much less certain that the manure thus collected and
prepared will be the means of making such other crops
as are grown more profitable than before.

Cottagers, or many of them, have the means of
growing Mushrooms, and thereby adding materially
to their too limited incomes. By cottagers is meant
more particularly those small holders of land which is
worked by one or two horses, and whose live stock may
consist of a couple of cows, half a score of sheep, and
half a hundred fowls. In some districts these hard-
working individuals are termed yeomen, in others small
farmers ; they are, however, extensively described as
" cottagers," and by that term are distinguished from

---

* For particulars of growing Mustard and Cress for market, and
cost and profit of culture, see the paper of Mr. L. Castle in the
Journal of Horticulture, page 209, March 16, 1882,

ordinary labourers. There are no men more industrious, more frugal, and who strive more earnestly to make both ends meet than respectable members of the class under notice, and not a few of them are enterprising and intelligent—at least, so parliamentary candidates say on certain occasions, if they are "correctly reported." These cottagers, among other things, contrive to make poultry pay ; in fact, were it not for the weekly sales of eggs and birds in the markets, they would often be uncomfortably short of ready money. These men are not as a rule devoted readers of current literature, and seldom speculate to a greater extent than a penny a week in a local newspaper. They know nothing whatever of Mushroom culture, have never heard of it as an industry ; but if its advantages were brought before them, and they were encouraged to give their attention to it and taught to become competent in it, nothing is more certain than that they might realise more ready money by it than it is possible by rearing poultry, although this should not be neglected. A well-conducted system of growing eggs will pay at times well, but an equally well-conducted method of growing Mushrooms will pay better ; and those who have a supply of manure, or can obtain it, and will make the best of it, and who are at the same time in the habit of taking or sending the produce of their holdings to market weekly, will find the advantage of including Mushrooms in their weekly supplies greater than they have imagined, and after the crops are disposed of they will still have the manure for their land. It is submitted, therefore, that the crop under notice is deserving of the attention of this large industrial section of the community.

Professional Gardeners, as a rule, are by no means well acquainted with the outdoor system of Mushroom culture. A vast number of them have never seen the method practised, and consequently not a few are somewhat incredulous on the subject. The accuracy of the records that are occasionally published in the press are doubted, or at least the results that are tabulated are considered as being exaggerated. Yet there are some gardeners (those who have had the advantage of deriving knowledge from the London market gardens, and most valuable is the practice that has been obtained there), know perfectly well that even greater crops can be gathered than those previously mentioned, and they will admit that the simplest and most profitable of all methods of growing Mushrooms is that which is practised of growing them on beds in the open air.

Landowners, Clergymen, and Professional Men who keep horses may readily procure a supply of Mushrooms in their gardens, and they will at the same time be preparing the manure for producing ordinary outdoor crops. If this great and important section of the community, established in every parish in the land, and ever anxious to improve the condition of their humbler neighbours, would bring their intelligence to bear in cultivating the crop in question, and produce what has been termed "object lessons" in the work, there could be little doubt that their example would be followed, the resources of their districts would be developed, and those who made themselves competent as Mushroom growers would unquestionably derive benefits commensurate with the thought and labour expended in obtaining them. A crop that is capable of yielding such results as have been shown on incontestible authority to have been produced, is unquestionably worthy of being introduced to the notice of those who are dependant for their livelihood on the production of the small plots of land pertaining to their holdings ; and a mode of utilising stable manure that in at least a million instances lies barren for months, can scarcely fail to commend itself to the attention of those who are interested in a subject of this nature.

OTHER EDIBLE FUNGI.

DURING the publication of several of the preceding
chapters in serial form many letters have been received
of an encouraging character, and suggestions have been
made and information imparted which are incorporated
in the work. One of not the least valued and important communications demands insertion in its
entirety. Mr. F. W. Burbidge, the accomplished
Curator of the Trinity College Botanic Gardens,
Dublin, writes as follows :—

"Your articles on Mushroom culture are very remarkable, and the
fresh originality of them has been appreciated by many besides myself.
They bear the impress of being true records of sound practice and
close research. They are, in truth, most suggestive articles, and I am
very glad to find that you are going to publish them in a separate
form. So reproduced they will prove useful to all Mushroom growers,
old or young.

"Only one little addition to your papers seems to me essential—a
paper suggesting the systematic culture of well-known edible fungi
other than the common Agaricus campestris. I am not aware that
anyone has experimented with the mycelium of other edible fungi ;
but seeing that there *are* some others—the Parasol Agaric (A. pro-
cerus) for example, equally as palatable and even more nutritious
than the common Mushroom—there here seems to be an open field for
progress.

"The Champignon, Chantarelle, the Fistulini, and some Boleti—
even the common Puff-ball when young—are food-yielding kinds,
which even if not as deserving of culture as is the milk-white
Mushroom of our meadows, yet deserve a better fate than total
neglect ! So far those delicious morsels the Truffles have defied
culture, although the late Mr. Tillery did obtain a partial success in
growing them when at Welbeck.

"The first step is to obtain spawn of these various kinds, and then
to attempt its cultural development. If we can obtain a supply of
spawn of the best edible fungi prepared on the same or on a similar
plan to that adopted in the case of the common Mushroom, we shall be
on a fair way towards our object, and may then look forward to fungi
being more generally grown and eaten as food rich in nitrogen, and
peculiarly delicate and toothsome in flavour.

"In the general use of the many different kinds of edible fungi we
are far behind the natives of Russia and other countries of North
Europe, where nearly all kinds, poisonous or not, are used in immense
quantities, being preserved in tubs of salt and vinegar—a course of

preservation which neutralises the deleterious properties of even those considered by us as the most poisonous kinds.

"First attempts in the preparation of spawn and in its after culture may not succeed, but energy and experience conquers all things, and the general culture of *the best* of our indigenous fungi is a subject which appears to me to be well worth attention."

The "little addition" indicated by Mr. Burbidge could not have been made in a better manner than he had made it himself. Without doubt those and other fungi are wholesome and delicious, but a long time must necessarily elapse before any of them can become so readily cultivable and really serviceable as the common Mushroom. The chief object in view is to increase the supply of an article of food that can with certainty be produced in this country to the benefit of cultivators and the satisfaction of consumers, for neither of them at present, except in a few solitary instances, obtains half a sufficient quantity of the much-coveted Mushrooms of the meadows. Yet it is most desirable that other kinds of edible fungi be brought under cultivation, and if samples of any of them can be sent to the publishing office of this work, together with their spawn or mycelium and a narration of the precise conditions under which it was produced, every effort shall be made to "fix" it after the manner of ordinary Mushroom spawn. This is the most practical way of expressing approval of the suggestion that has been made.

THE PROSPECTIVE SUPPLY OF MUSHROOMS.

AFTER what has been said in the foregoing pages it may not unnaturally be supposed that if a great number of persons engage in the work of Mushroom culture the supply of produce will exceed the demand. There is no substantial reason for this opinion ; on the contrary, it is much more likely that an increased supply will create a still greater demand, as has been the case with many other articles that meet the public taste. The present average prices may not always be maintained, but that will be a distinct advantage to consumers, while the growers by large sales may expect to be adequately remunerated. When tea and newspapers were much more costly than now, and the profits on each ounce of the former and sheet of the latter greater, the returns to the vendors from their aggregate sales bore no comparison with those that followed when the necessities of life indicated were cheapened and brought within the means of an enormously enlarged constituency of purchasers. At the present time it must be remembered that the Mushroom supply of this country is utterly inadequate for consumptive purposes, as witness the millions of tins of preserved Mushrooms that are imported chiefly from France. In the *Journal of Horticulture,* vol. xxxv., page 48, it is stated that "The daily production of Mushrooms in and around Paris when the beds are in full profit is 25 tons. The Mushroom caves, together with the beds in the market gardens, not only supply the Paris markets, but large quantities are exported to England and other parts of Europe, one house alone in Paris sending 14,000 boxes annually to London. A single French firm used over 200 tons of Mushrooms per annum, mostly for preserving." Why should not the Mushroom-producing resources of this country be similarly developed, and as is suggested on the first page of this manual, England be able to export instead of continually importing an article of food that can be grown so abundantly and well ?

Again, why should not a bountiful supply of Mushroom ketchup—pure, honest, genuine, unadulterated ketchup—be obtainable ? At the present time the great bulk of what is sold as ketchup is a mysterious compound nearly innocent of Mushrooms, and is not always wholly composed of vegetable products, since bullock's liver is an active ingredient in its manufacture. The public have a right to expect something better than this. Pure ketchup is always in demand, and there is an open market for ten thousand times more than can at present be offered. If, therefore, the supply of Mushrooms for ordinary culinary purposes should be excessive during the six months November to April, both inclusive, of which the probability is extremely remote, the successful cultivator can not only insure himself against loss, but realise a fair profit by the manufacture of ketchup, for it is not generally known that Mushroom-growing well conducted on the system described in the foregoing pages is lucrative even if the whole produce is " melted down " into this favourite condiment.

ENEMIES OF MUSHROOMS.

Slugs and snails are often very annoying. If the beds are carefully examined at night with the aid of a lantern in all probability a number of the depredators may be caught and destroyed. Heaps of brewers grains or bran placed near the beds will, if examined after dark, often be found covered with snails, and if these in turn be covered with salt they will do no further damage. Woodlice are occasionally troublesome ; pieces of parsnip boiled in a solution of arsenic are readily eaten by them, and this forms their last meal. The poisoned baits should be placed in small flower pots and must be kept from fowls. In houses Mushrooms when approaching the size of walnuts sometimes cease swelling and rot, becoming very offensive. This is caused by a fungus, Xylaria vaporaria, which takes possession of them, and can only be eradicated by clearing out the beds and thoroughly cleansing, limewashing, and disinfecting the house. It is usually introduced with particles of unpurified manure ; it is very destructive, but fortunately not prevalent on beds in the open air.

CONCLUSION.

In the preparation of this treatise endeavour has been made to give the several details of culture by which alone success can be achieved. Trivial some points may appear to the uninitiated, but the experienced cultivator will recognise their importance. It is by attention to small matters that great results are accomplished, and the advice that was given to the writer many years ago by one of the greatest and best of men in the ranks of horticulture, and found useful, indeed most valuable, may not inappropriately be given to others, as, to the young especially, it may prove useful too. " In whatever you do," said Mr. G. W. Johnson, the founder and late Co-Editor of the *Journal of Horticulture*, " either in writing or working, do not ignore the simplicities that bear on your object, but attend to what are termed small matters. . . . . . . ' I promote,' said Napoleon, ' the man who is capable of mastering small details; any elephant can lift a hundredweight, few can pick up a pin.' " Let that advice be followed, and the sentiment be remembered by all who wish to excel ; it applies strictly to the subject in question. Master the small matters, and what is truly great will be attained— success.

Lightning Source UK Ltd.
Milton Keynes UK
UKHW010637081118
331980UK00001B/12/P